What people

The End (

It's rare to find a book th   ...... or the recent history of global politics, but the Aufhebunga Bunga boys have produced just such a text. The authors take us through a series of political upheavals and popular protests, populism, post-politics and anti-politics, and the defeats of Bernie Sanders and Jeremy Corbyn, in eight short bracing chapters. The authors offer original and critical insights into the campaigns against corruption in countries around the world, from Hungary to Brazil, to the case study of Silvio Berlusconi in Italy. Engaged, informed, ordinary and discontent, self-educated, puzzled, disgusted and even a little angry, the reader for whom this book is written will be able to engage with the authors' project of conceptual mapping and left-wing self-critique. Despite the darkness of the times, the book will give you a sliver of hope. It's a page turner as one wonders how the authors will lead us to that tiny ray of light: socialist Enlightenment.

Catherine Liu, Professor of Film and Media Studies/Visual Studies, UC Irvine

Suddenly we find ourselves thrown into a time of chaos and confusion, breakdown and decline. This short, smart book navigates a terrain of ideological mystification and encourages us to take a sober look at the balance of forces going into this tumultuous period, waking from the boredom of the end of history.

Angela Nagle, author, *Kill All Normies*

In this provocative volume, the crew behind Aufhebunga Bunga podcast surveys the political landscape at "end of the end of history". Looking at the triumph of neoliberalism and its tug-of-war with its populist Doppelgänger in different countries – from the US to the UK, from Italy to Brazil – the authors vividly demonstrate that, while neoliberalism's contradictions are plainly visible, the Left is incapable of responding to a profound crisis of authority. A must-read for all those willing to gaze into the depths of contemporary ideological and cultural wars.

Paolo Gerbaudo, Director of the Centre for Digital Culture, King's College London; author, *The Digital Party*

The End of the End of History

Politics in the Twenty-First Century

The End of the End of History

Politics in the Twenty-First Century

Alex Hochuli, George Hoare,
Philip Cunliffe

Winchester, UK
Washington, USA

JOHN HUNT PUBLISHING

First published by Zero Books, 2021
Zero Books is an imprint of John Hunt Publishing Ltd., No. 3 East St., Alresford,
Hampshire SO24 9EE, UK
office@jhpbooks.com
www.johnhuntpublishing.com
www.zero-books.net

For distributor details and how to order please visit the 'Ordering' section on our website.

ISBN: 978 1 78904 523 9
978 1 78904 524 6 (ebook)
Library of Congress Control Number: 2020942261

A CIP catalogue record for this book is available from the British Library.

Design: Stuart Davies

UK: Printed and bound by CPI Group (UK) Ltd, Croydon, CR0 4YY
Printed in North America by CPI GPS partners

We operate a distinctive and ethical publishing philosophy in
all areas of our business, from our global network of authors to
production and worldwide distribution.

Contents

Also by Philip Cunliffe

Lenin Lives! Zero Books, ISBN: 978-1-78535-697-1

Acknowledgments

As with so many young men of our generation, tragically we were driven to start a podcast. Having come of age in the political wasteland of the 2000s, the turbulence of the mid-2010s felt energizing: the return of politics! When we started Aufhebunga Bunga in April 2017, we didn't have a clear idea of what we wanted to achieve, though the idea that the tedious End of History might finally be ending was a shared premise. As the podcast developed, we decided to task ourselves more explicitly with exploring the emerging age's contours.

We owe thanks, firstly, to friend of the podcast Lee Jones for encouraging us in mid-2019 to write this book. The undergraduate course Lee conceived and teaches at Queen Mary, University of London – Politics at the End of the End of History – was a further spur to develop the framework that had emerged in producing the podcast.

Gratitude is also owed to Catherine Liu for her continuing enthusiasm, and for inviting us to UC Irvine to record and participate in her graduate seminar critiquing "wellness". Our "CaliBunga" series on the Californian ideology was a product of that trip, and helped further cement our perspective.

A huge thanks to all those who read and provided invaluable comments on chapter drafts: Benjamin Bradlow, Benjamin Fogel, Paolo Gerbaudo, Abby Gilbert, Lee Jones, Euan Marshall, Andresa Medeiros, Dan Taylor, Matthew Thompson, Sally Turner.

To all our podcast guests over the years: we owe you a significant debt of gratitude for your time and for participating in what continue to prove hugely enriching exchanges (for us, and hopefully for yourselves and the listeners). The conversations have certainly helped broaden and deepen our understanding of the strange times in which we find ourselves.

Thanks also to Jonny Mundey (jonnymundey.com) for creating our theme music and Dewi Gonzalez (ramune.io) for designing our logo.

And finally, a massive thanks to all our listeners and especially to our subscribers/patrons.

Needless to say, responsibility for all that is contained herein is ours alone.

Chapter 1

Introduction

Bat soup. Xenophobic insinuations. Toppled statues. Hazmat suits. Bizarre weather events. Wildfire riots. Improvised police states. Mass quarantine.

The strange end times we find ourselves in are more like a B-Movie apocalypse than the orderly sequence of "events" found in history books. But the weirdness of contemporary life is not only a product of the Covid-19 crisis. If we look at the doomy memes about 2021, we see they are functionally identical to ones from 2020, 2019 – or 2016 for that matter. Indeed, remember when all those Boomer celebrities started dying[1] in the same year as that failed Turkish coup, random Jihadist terror across Europe, the Zika outbreak, Trump's victory and the Brexit vote? Those days when everyone dug up that Lenin quotation about decades where nothing happens and weeks where decades happen?

This was the End of the End of History. It was announced in 2016. 2020 made it definitive.

We stand at a pivotal moment. Amid the chaos, states of emergency and extraordinary state responses, we are undergoing an epochal political shift. The richest and most powerful states in the West are fumbling their way out of neoliberalism. Such regime change had almost been forgotten as a possibility – unless it was applied at the end of a gun in distant lands.

Or at least, we thought that if regime change were to happen, it would be different. The coronavirus outbreak coincided with the undoing of a surge of left-wing attempts to gain state power. The defeat of Jeremy Corbyn's Labour Party and the collapse of Bernie Sanders' campaign for president came within 4 months of each other, either side of the initial lockdowns. These attempts, called "left-populism," aimed to move beyond neoliberalism, to

1

defend welfare, and to create a new, collective and egalitarian politics. They felt promising; they made it feel like maybe politics was back, after a long time away.

The failure of left-populism, strangely, happened at the same time as right-wing governments adopted policies that strongly departed from neoliberal orthodoxy. Donald Trump passed a $3tn stimulus package, while Boris Johnson's government announced £100bn in extra spending to pay 80 percent of wages and support the self-employed. Policies the Left had been proposing were recuperated by the Right, and this was done at just the moment of the greatest popular demobilization in history: the lockdowns. There is deep irony to this, since one of the main problems with left-populism was that it had tried to do socialism without the masses.

Societies have been withdrawing from politics for some time; over the past decades, trade unions, political parties and civic organizations have all become empty shells.[2] The inevitable consequence was that things became steadily worse. But for a while, nothing major seemed to change. Globalization meant harmony and growth – at least, on the surface.

Then, suddenly, the world slipped out of control. Crisis was back. But with the masses only playing a bit-part, it all became deranged; politics fluctuated wildly, unanchored from the great agglomeration of people within political organizations that had characterized much of the twentieth century. But at least the craziness made people think about politics again.

To grasp the notion that *politics was back*, and to understand the profound sense of disorder that is a feature of our age, we need to go back to the End of History. This was the period after the fall of the Berlin Wall in November 1989, which marked the symbolic end of a world divided between communism and capitalism, and the total victory of the latter. Only when we recall the tedium of the age known as the End of History – that sense that staid neoliberal democracy was all there was – can we grasp how shocking the return of politics since 2016 has been.

1.1 I hate myself and I want to buy

Reflecting on the dawn of a new era in the early 1990s, the historian Eric Hobsbawm noted that the "short twentieth century" "ended in a global disorder whose nature was unclear, and without an obvious mechanism for either ending it or keeping it under control."[3] This impotence was not, however, only due to the complexity of the problems themselves. After all, talking-up complexity is the trick technocrats have been pulling for 3 decades, with the sole purpose of lowering expectations. Rather, the impotence lay "in the apparent failure of all programs, old and new, for managing or improving the affairs of the human race."[4]

Moreover, we were left with no force even promising to do so. Surveying the scene, Hobsbawm observed a world divided between "stable, strong and favored states [that] might think themselves immune from the insecurity and carnage," and those found outside the Western bubble. However, various new threats were on the horizon – terrorism, Islamic fundamentalism, mass migration, environmental degradation and so on – that might come to puncture that bubble.

Outside, in what was still being called the "Third World," albeit by then anachronistically, there were various movements that did not hold to the universalizing ideals that structured the Cold War conflict (liberal capitalism or communism). Instead, these movements sought merely a secure identity and social order in a disintegrating world; ethnic- or religious-based movements proliferated. These might even succeed in overthrowing regimes, Hobsbawm noted, but, like the interwar fascism that also revolted against modern dissolution, they had no real solutions to problems. Worse – because this applied the world over, to all political organizations, it was not even clear that political ideas were capable of generating organized national mass movements.

For their part, citizens largely seemed resigned to leave affairs of the state to the "political class." What proliferated in the wake of this withdrawal was an "amalgam of slogans and emotions" that could barely be called ideology: identity politics and xenophobia.

So, what has changed since 1994 when Hobsbawm's work was first published? The disorder is only too apparent now, and movements for "secure identity and social order" seem an adequate descriptor for the political forces that rule many Western nations, such as national-populism. But to see only uninterrupted disorder would be to ignore precisely the settled order that governed the End of History era. Sure, there were "new threats," but none that would put into question liberal democracy, precisely because the new threats did not carry any serious program for an alternative and better means of organizing society. The New World Order pronounced by President George HW Bush in 1991 promised peace and cooperation under the aegis of American leadership – indeed, its total hegemony. But it was not only in geopolitical terms that stability would be achieved. The whole way that national politics operated was premised on the withdrawal of the citizenry from active engagement. In its place was "post-politics," a form of government that tries to foreclose political contestation by emphasizing consensus, "eradicating" ideology and ruling by recourse to evidence and expertise rather than interests or ideals. Underpinning all this was an economic regime – neoliberalism – that privileged private competition above everything else. The state's role was merely to regulate market exchanges and to ensure the latter's proper functioning. Ever-expanding and untrammeled international commerce – globalization – would provide a bounty to the winners. And really, everyone would be a winner: a rising tide lifts all boats.

This notion had such success that it naturalized economic relations. The big questions, about what is produced and who gets how much, were settled. Politics, then, had little to attend to, and accordingly the state's capacities atrophied. With nothing to fight over, citizens withdrew from the public realm, to focus on their private affairs. It seemed as if Hobsbawm's Age of Extremes had given way to a different age, the Age of the Self.[5] Pursuing your private desires in the market was the sum total of human experience. The victor of the twentieth century ideological struggle between communism and capitalism was, in fact, consumerism – "the 'ism' that won."[6]

Of course, it was capitalism that really won. But shorn of a systemic alternative, even the notion that we lived in a system called "capitalism" receded from view. Contemporary society came to be seen as a natural order instead of the product of conflictual historical development. That was, until the 2007-08 Global Financial Crisis (GFC). Then, suddenly, this autonomous thing we referred to as "the economy" was called into question. That event marked the first major interruption to the "End of History" proclaimed by Francis Fukuyama in 1989 upon the collapse of "really existing socialism." Events seemed to accelerate. But even so, it took a little while for the dislocations of the GFC to find conscious political manifestation.

The early 2010s saw protests, new movements and even (failed) revolutions. But the real denouement, for the centers of global capitalism, arrived in 2016. The election of Donald Trump and the victory of Leave in the EU referendum in Britain marked the end to any complacency about the permanence of prevailing models of liberal democracy, globalization or neoliberalism. Those events were the most prominent instances of the most important force that arose to challenge the post-political consensus: *anti-politics*.

In various spots around the world, including in the nerve-centers of global capitalism, people were proclaiming "they do not represent us!" The neoliberal establishments that held court in most of the world were shaken. The authority of practices as varied as journalism, economics and the law also became corroded due to declining credibility. The yawning trust deficit that characterized so much social and political discourse was a product of the instrumentalization of expertise during the End of History. Managerial technocracy purported to have the answers, but it was fatally damaged, first by the GFC and then by Trump and Brexit in 2016.

The 4 years that followed were marked by precisely that sense of disorder to which Hobsbawm testified in the early days following the collapse of the Soviet Union. A global revolt against political establishments was now underway, and those who identified with the crumbling order were losing their minds, while grasping for outré conspiracy theories to explain what was happening. How could our gleaming, frictionless and over-lit landscape be overshadowed, how could there be such darkness at noon? Was the End of History to be eclipsed?

Should there have been any doubt, the Covid-19 crisis of 2020 proved definitive, the End of the End of History was before us. History ended in 1989. In 2008, the economic order was shaken. The political reckoning arrived in 2016. By 2020, the End of History was over.

1.2 A billion balconies facing the sun

The epochal nature of these transformations can only fully be grasped by recalling the affective landscape of the End of History. What did that culture *feel* like? As alternative political visions faded, culture – especially "alternative culture" – seemed to float freely, unmoored from any determinate social perspective. So, consumerism ruled, with alternative culture's attacks on it only proving their target's real dominance. And if attacking it failed, you could just stop caring. The End of History was the age of consumerism, yes, but it was also an age of nihilism.

In the early days of this era, techno music and rave culture bloomed. The world felt open and full of possibility, at least for oneself as an individual. It was almost as if old public duties and strictures were being shaken off. The repetitiveness of dance music seemed to exemplify something of the age: house music and techno had no beginning, middle and end; it was all about texture and feeling, not narrative structure. These styles appeared to recapitulate the point about the "end of grand narratives," the defining feature of postmodernity.[7] "Alternative" rock similarly seemed to go nowhere. Kurt Cobain of Nirvana was fatally aware of his own "precorporation" – the realization of being a cliché of opposition in the culture of spectacle.[8] The veteran music critic Greil Marcus heard in the band's music "the feeling of humiliation, disintegration and defeat by some distant malevolence." The countercultural stance in the 1990s went by the name "attitude," but really its function was "to proclaim one's own limitations loudly and to dismiss the possibility of going beyond them."[9] Even hip-hop was fast abandoning its impetus for social change in favor of bling, bitches and guns; Public Enemy gave way to Jay-Z, and then to Kanye West and 6ix9ine. In the UK, Britpop seemed to make the country cool again and the Union Jack – previously thought to be a symbol of racism and imperialism – could be waved with levity, embraced by pop culture icons (who were soon to be invited to Downing Street anyway).

Meanwhile, mainstream cinema featured outbursts of mindless and mostly depoliticized violence, in response to consumerist ennui (even when they purported to be critiques of such), in films such as *Fight Club, Natural Born Killers* or *Falling Down*. The "distant malevolence" that Marcus observed in grunge found reflection in movies that transmitted paranoid themes of total simulacrum or mind control, such as *The Matrix*, most obviously, as well as *The Truman Show* and *Existenz*.

Television, *the* medium of the 1990s, could still occasionally act as a vehicle for transgression, even while it was being slated as the "idiot box" by what remained of the counterculture. *The*

Simpsons and *Beavis & Butthead*, both tied to "alt" culture, soon led to *Family Guy* and *South Park*, both of which tried to push mainstream offensiveness to the limit, though the link to youth subcultures was increasingly tenuous. Emblematic of television of the early 2000s was *Jackass*, presaging a world of self-made celebrities and YouTube stars. It was superficially subversive but definitely apolitical, with similarly little connection to youth subculture, other than skateboarding. The masochistic antics of the *Jackass* crew seemed a nihilistic attempt to overcome boredom. And if self-punishment wasn't your bag, then you could indulge in the humiliation of the other: *Big Brother, Jerry Springer, Jeremy Kyle, I'm a Celebrity* and a range of other "reality" TV programs allowed for the elevation of the self through the sadistic denigration of the stranger.

Stylistically, the waves of "retro" and the appropriation and rehashing of the fashion of previous micro-eras began to accelerate. Early 1990s rave culture and its "Second Summer of Love" looked to the late 60s for inspiration, and was followed in quick succession by a fascination with the 70s. The popular catchphrase of the time, "it's the 90s" (meaning "get with it") strove to demonstrate modernity, in spite of the era's evident fixation on hipper pasts.

For those with a sense of what politics had been or might be again – or those who merely held hopes that politics might be interesting and angry and rebellious and romantic – the rap metal of Rage Against the Machine and the documentaries of Michael Moore were made to fill the void. But as society as a whole became depoliticized, these "political" artifacts stood out as hyper-political attempts to energize the masses through sheer force of will. They naturally failed. Worse, they were just another identity or – to be truly damning – brand.

The lack of a sense of a future, the eternal present of those decades, meant conceptions of History changed. Mark Fisher acutely named the predominant mood "depressive hedonia."[10]

It was not so much that people could not experience pleasure, rather that they evinced an inability to do anything *other* than pursue pleasure. Consumerism and nihilism. Something was missing. Society had retired; we had gone home to sit listlessly on our balconies. We had waved "a final goodbye to wars and ideologies. But," asked novelist JG Ballard in *Cocaine Nights*, "how do you energize people, give them some sense of community? A world lying on its back is vulnerable to any cunning predator."[11]

A sense of community was sought in escapist and hedonistic adventures like rave culture, which pretended to stand for "resistance," but only in the most temporary sense. Its political correlate was in the global justice movement (also known as anti- or alter-globalization), and later on, Occupy. Protest approximated carnival: it would overturn or destroy hierarchies, but things would return to consumerist normality the next day. Protest and dance both provided little more than a release valve.

The pre-internet (really, pre-social media) culture of the 1990s and early 2000s represented the last embers of the counterculture,[12] an antagonistic stance toward the mainstream and bourgeois. It was a facet of the so-called "artistic" critique of capitalism that strove for liberation and rejected inauthenticity.[13] Of course, shards of an oppositional culture could still be found. The music-sharing software Napster, for instance, provided a focal point for debates around ownership, copyright and access. Looking back, though, these references seem like artifacts of a passed cultural moment and, in an unfortunate irony, a victim of what Simon Reynolds termed "retromania."[14] Contemporary revivals of earlier pop culture moments rehash the style but without even the limited social content of the 1990s. The "artistic critique" has been fully incorporated by capitalism.

1.3 The wave pool

What was oppositional politics like then, during the End of History? Until the September 11 attacks, which shifted attention to war and geopolitics, left-wing activism took on a neo-anarchist bent. Events and movements such as the Carnival Against Capitalism, Reclaim the Streets and Tute Bianche replaced organization, programs and leadership with set-piece confrontations with the police. A quasi-revival of situationism featured tactics such as "adbusting," attempts to critique consumerism by defacing advertisements. Rather than focus on production and distribution, the neo-situationists tilted at capitalist windmills in their narrow focus on the mediatized "spectacle." The idea that defacing brands provided injury to the capitalist system was premised on the idea that the old, upstanding bourgeois authority was still there, and would be offended. But your granddad's capitalism was long gone. In fact, advertisers were already using the same techniques to sell images back to "alternative" consumers. Long before Kendall Jenner's Pepsi ads regurgitated Black Lives Matter protests, beat writer William S. Burroughs was hawking sportswear in a 1994 Nike spot.

The supposedly more serious alternative politics of the time, inspired by Naomi Klein's *No Logo* (1999) and Hardt and Negri's *Empire* (2000), sought to unify a bewildering array of different struggles. The phrase "teamsters and turtles" signified the union of workers and environmentalists. But its organizational incoherence was reflected in its schizophrenic political messaging.

The archetypal embodiment of post-historical nihilism – the 9/11 attacks – then put an end to this wave of oppositional protest. The anti-war movement that emerged in opposition to the US-led invasion of Iraq seemed to indicate a new seriousness. Focus shifted from American brands to American foreign policy. And yet, protest only traded the carnivalesque for the moralistic. Despite millions on the street, it never felt like the war might be stopped. Indeed, perma-war continues to this day.

With the waning of anti-war protest, environmentalism

took up the slack. Unlike the late 1990s attempt at coalition-building, by the mid-2000s the workers were gone from the scene. Without even the pretense of roots in industrial production, environmentalism became fully oriented toward consumption. Instead of political activity in the interests of a collective self, 2000s environmentalism and humanitarianism were entirely other-oriented. What was the picture of the world they painted? Rich, greedy consumers in the Global North and poor, naturalized and needy producers in the Global South. And that was when advocacy was about people at all. At its worst, environmentalism positioned itself against humans altogether, unifying nihilism and (negative) consumerism.[15]

The moralization of consumers seemed the only point of leverage for "opposition" to capitalism. While in the 1990s, alternative culture maintained the pretense of being outside and against the market, by the 2000s, the market was the means through which politics was to be pursued. The writing was on the wall when the anti-consumerist *Adbusters* magazine decided to start selling their own "unbranded" Blackspot Shoes in 2004. Ethical or political consumerism flourished, with Fairtrade purporting to be "in and against" the market.[16] The Make Poverty History campaign in the middle of the decade, with its consumable white bracelets, was the pinnacle of doing politics for people "over there." Soon after, the growth of social media suggested new technologies could be handmaidens to political-consumer campaigns. The heavily moralistic tone and images of distant suffering were gradually eased out in favor of breezy entreaties to "just click": look how easy it is to enact positive change. Here was "clicktivism," when we believed social media would change the world for the better.

But the Global Financial Crisis soon brought politics home. Middle-class advocacy for faraway victims could no longer gain media attention in the age of home foreclosures and austerity. The farce of "Kony 2012" only confirmed the demise of this style of activism. Now, a new discourse on inequality sprung up, seizing on the divide between rich and poor at home. Here, maybe, was the embryo of a new class politics. Politics *by and for* the masses – rather than *by* middle-class do-gooders *for* worthy victims over there – was back.

But then, after Occupy, activist discourse underwent the most farcical revival of all. 1980s-style campus wars made a comeback as fourth-wave feminism. This superficial, white-collar radicalism soon expanded into intersectionality. All the energy from the new inequality politics seemed suddenly to be sucked into rancorous online culture wars. The young university students and graduates, who in the mid-2000s were to be found shouting at holidaymakers for unnecessary flying, were reincarnated in the mid-2010s as Twitter avatars telling normies that Halloween costumes were "not ok."

In short, the successive waves of activism since the end of the Cold War had become ever more individualistic and consumer-oriented; they had acquiesced to the market. Wave after wave crashed against the shore, but no transformation occurred. It might as well have been all for fun. None of it was serious about seizing state power.

1.4 Wedging open the future

But then, in a separate (though not wholly independent) development, a generation was returning to formal politics. The movements of the squares in Spain and Greece birthed new parties in Podemos and Syriza. The same subterranean forces led to the infusion of new, left-wing energy into decrepit parties in the UK and US. Indeed, it was this enthusiasm that led us to start a podcast, *Aufhebunga Bunga,* which generated many of the ideas in this book. After years of complaining about the absence of politics, things suddenly seemed to be happening. The old delusions of "changing the world without taking power" were being overcome; organizations were being built; everyone was suddenly a socialist. But just because the End of History was ending, it did not mean that something new was clearly presenting itself. Rather, the seeds of the new had still to be sought out.

Unfortunately, the winner of the late 2010s was not to be the Left. Instead, elites still ruled, even if there was a changing of the guard afoot. In tone, "populism" had the upper hand, provoking hysterical reactions from the liberal wing of the establishment. In substance, the ties between liberalism and democracy were straining. The model in the ascendant was China's – an authoritarian, state-led capitalism. This is a very different world. So, though the End of the End of History is providing a sudden political opening, the Left has thus far proved unable to seize it. Instead, mainstream politics is mutating to meet – however inadequately – the old, unresolved contradictions of the GFC

Table 1.1: Mainstream and oppositional politics from the Cold War until the present.

	Hegemonic political force	Dominant forms of left politics	Media	Oppositional culture	Political sentiment
Cold War (1945-1989)	Liberal democracy	Social democracy, Anti-imperialism, Communism	Newspaper & Television	Counterculture	Engagement, Opposition
End of History (1989-2015)	Post-politics	Anti-globalization, Social justice	Television	Commodification of counterculture, Depressive hedonism	Apathy
End of the End of History (2016 – ?)	Anti-politics	Left-populism	Internet, Social media	Memes	Anger

and the new ones prompted by the Covid-19 crisis. The new age will require a new Left.

What we aim to do here is to explore how the End of History ended – and what that means for politics today. Through analysis of these historical developments, we hope to develop a framework allowing us to tease out what is new and what is coming next. In the table above, we offer a schematic account of political transformations undergone from the Cold War through the End of History to today's period of the End of the End of History, which encapsulates the argumentative thread running through the book.

Many of the cases and examples we draw from are of the Anglophone world, because the global developments we trace express themselves there more clearly. The End of History was originally theorized from a North American and European perspective, and the core of the capitalist world around the North Atlantic remains the trendsetter (until now anyway; the Covid-19 crisis may prove to be China's "Sputnik moment").[17] However, we draw on examples from elsewhere in the world whenever possible in order to illustrate how the "End of History" and the "End of the End of History" schema applies globally. For instance, when discussing the politics of anti-corruption, we examine the case of Eastern Europe, since post-ideological politics emerged there starkly after the fall of really existing socialism; in one sense, it was where the model of liberal democracy was implanted earliest and with the greatest force at the End of History, and where revolt against it now stares us in the face.[18]

This isn't an exhaustive account of global politics today, not least because different nations and regions manifest specific inflections of the general, global tendencies on which we concentrate. For instance, China rises during the End of History, but in ways that run counter to neoliberal prescriptions; Brazil saw the emergence of the last great mass social-democratic party in the late 1980s, ruling through the 2000s; Germany's hegemonic position in the EU means it hasn't seen the popular movements that seized Southern Europe. And, of course, outside the Western bubble, politics may have seemed much more alive than in our Anglosphere-driven characterizations above. There were protests and riots and coups, and a wider variety of regimes. But mainly, it was just capitalism, redder in tooth and claw than in the core, as it has always been.

The crucial point is that extremely few cases pointed toward a radically different form of social organization in the way socialism, radical revolt and communism did throughout the twentieth century. Indeed, the exceptions prove the rule. Witness the Western Left's fixation on Palestine, Venezuela or more recently Rojava (combined population today: 40 million). Morose societies in the West led us to search corners of the world for green shoots. But politics always begins at home.

1.5 Outline of the book

Essential to the theoretical framework of this book is the understanding that various twenty-first century experiments have not, so far, amounted to History with a capital "H." Francis Fukuyama was ridiculed repeatedly for his infamous prediction, which only demonstrated that few had actually read him. The proposition was not that there would be no more events, or that every society would conform to that of Western liberal democracy. There was a more profound sense of History, a dialectic of universal human struggles for freedom – it was *that* which would be missing. Hence Fukuyama's gloom, not triumphalism, in announcing the new age. How the End of History is ending, but has not led to a restart of History proper, is the subject of Chapter 2.

If History is not quite back, what about politics? Chapter 3 centers on the question of its return. Politics was negated during the End of History through a strategy of depoliticization known as "post-politics." How did it operate and what made it come apart? If *apathy* ruled the 1990s and 2000s, then does the prevalence of *anger* in our current period signify something new? We argue that the challenger to post-politics is *anti-politics* – a rejection of the political establishment and its managerial approach to governing society. Anti-politics, by challenging consensus with dissensus (or division), brings politics back in.

In Chapter 4, we turn to a collection of psycho-political reactions to the End of the End of History that we call Neoliberal Order Breakdown Syndrome. The return of political divisions, of us and them, or of the people and the elite, rattled an arrangement that had proved very comfortable for many in the media, NGOs, the academy or the civil service. The popular rejection of the authority of "politics knowers," in particular, prompted a range of symptomatic behaviors, from denial of social change to repetition compulsion, which we catalog and discuss.

In Chapter 5, we examine the predominant political force in the world today, the one shaking political establishments: anti-politics. Through an account of various cases around the world, from anti-corruption to populism to "horizontalism," we show how anti-politics purports to be popular and democratizing, but in fact contains a self-defeating logic: by attacking political authority and rejecting representation, anti-politics prevents popular movements from seizing power for themselves. Even worse, anti-politics can be depoliticizing, either leading back to post-political management, or paving the way for authoritarian rule. Brazil's experience with anti-corruption politics is explored in depth as an illustrative example of these tendencies.

But Brazil's drama was merely a farcical re-enactment of Italy's pioneering tragedy, the subject of Chapter 6. Italy's experience in the 1990s and 2000s is instructive: it is an augury of the global End of History, and its ending. In Silvio Berlusconi we have the archetypal politician of the age: a media mogul, a neoliberal manager, both a populist everyman and hyper-successful Übermensch, a beneficiary of anti-corruption politics and an avatar of political corruption. Further, Italy itself condenses so many contemporary trends: regional inequality, economic stagnation, emigration and hostility to immigration, implanted technocratic governments and EU austerity. Italy is also a pioneer in a new form of political organization: techno-populism, a fusion of the two main trends of the End of History. Political forms are the subject of Chapter 7, in which the analysis advanced in the preceding chapters is applied, firstly, to parties, examining how they have been hollowed out and reshaped. Secondly, we look to protest, which, contrary to popular belief, never really went away. Instead, different forms of protest became more prominent, even as politics was emptied of popular passions. Key here are changing class dynamics and the way higher education has become a new social cleavage. Younger cohorts of professional and managerial strata of society have remained politicized – and recently become even more so. This explains not just enthusiasm for protest, but also the prevalence of angry culture wars today. Sadly, much of what now passes for popular politics in our new age is merely antagonism between two factions of the middle class.

So is politics back? Perhaps...but in strange forms. The mutations in political ideologies – and the class alignments they presuppose – are analyzed in Chapter 8. In this speculative section of the book, we offer prognoses on how a post-Covid-19 world will polarize politically. With the traditional managers of capitalism abandoning the strictures of neoliberalism, a revamped corporatist arrangement emerges. Ironically, it is the forces of the liberal Center-Left that will become the last standard-bearers of the neoliberal package – especially its political and cultural aspects: technocracy, managerialism, intersectionality and individualism. The post-neoliberal world will also see the continuing growth of a defensive and xenophobic vision of society on the Right. This organicist conception of the nation will be Malthusian, fixated on surplus populations and limited resources.

We conclude by discussing what new forms popular and working-class politics may take. The stakes are growing. The lotus-eating End of History is receding quickly. Transcending the age in which the people stay home, politics runs on autopilot and the elite abandons itself to bunga-bunga parties is of the utmost necessity.

Chapter 2

The Ends of History

How did the End of History end, and why did history not restart? What does it even mean to say that history ends? As time is irreversible, how could history end?

In our contemporary era, the molding of political and social history into a coherent narrative structure – one that could conceivably have a beginning, a middle and, crucially, an end – stems back to the end of the Cold War. In 1989, an academic functionary and political scientist of the US security state, Francis Fukuyama, claimed that Western victory in the Cold War not only brought one particular period of international history to a close but brought an end to the narrative itself. Fukuyama's strange and striking thesis – which was in turn inspired by the philosophy of German idealism as developed by GWF Hegel, writing in the aftermath of the Napoleonic Wars during the early nineteenth century – was immediately challenged, criticized and repulsed on every front. Fukuyama himself balked, lost his nerve and eventually retreated from certain aspects of his argument in response to the multiple intellectual assaults that he sustained.

Fukuyama qualified his thesis in the wake of the disastrous invasion of Iraq at the start of the twenty-first century, and then modulated it further in response to the British vote to withdraw from the European Union (EU) in 2016 and the election of Donald Trump as US president later that same year. Even as history seemed to take a dramatic new turn, no one – not even Fukuyama himself – was willing to stand for the claim that history had identifiable and meaningful patterns that gave an underlying shape to the flow of events – despite the clear evidence through which Fukuyama's thesis was vindicated over and over again.

What did it mean, then, for history to end when the Berlin

Wall crumbled in 1989, and the USSR itself was dissolved by 1992? When Fukuyama said in his 1989 article in *The National Interest* that history had ended, it was more than a flourish to glorify the providential American victory over the USSR in a decades-long struggle.[1] Rather, Fukuyama was saying that the Cold War was about much more than a balance of power, diplomatic stratagems, competing alliance systems or counting who had the most nuclear rockets and tanks. By saying that history had ended, Fukuyama was saying that the Cold War was ultimately what it appeared to be: a struggle between competing ideological systems over what was the best means for organizing human society for the future. In other words, the competing ideologies of the Cold War were not merely camouflage for the interests of state power, but were central to the conflict itself. If we take Fukuyama's thesis seriously, then, it would mean that beneath the hypocrisy, malevolence and broken promises of the "Free World," and the even more mangled hopes embodied in Soviet Communism, the struggle over the best means of organizing society was a real one.

As already indicated, Fukuyama's idea was not original – he took it from the European planner and Franco-Russian émigré philosopher Alexandre Kojève, who in turn cribbed it from Hegel's post-Napoleonic political philosophy. How did Fukuyama transplant a thesis taken from early nineteenth century Germany to postwar Europe, and then to the post-Cold War world? Fukuyama's Hegelian flourishes were widely seen as the seal on the American victory, the vindication of American government and the American system, and ultimately the vindication of American empire itself – endowing US efforts at democratization with historic inevitability and finality. The clear, hard claim of the thesis was that US victory in the Cold War resolved the basic questions of human government.

The Cold War had always been a global conflict. This meant that virtually every country, every political party, every government and every rebel group – no matter how trivial and of whatever ideological stripe – had to decide how they related to the US-Soviet clash, even if only to opt out of it. In so doing, they all, in turn, participated in and helped solidify and globalize the Cold War.[2] Who were your allies and enemies? Who was going to provide you with weapons – Washington, Moscow or Beijing? What was your social and economic program going to be once you were in power? Who would support you at the United Nations and in world diplomacy? Who would finance your economic development? Who would you trade with? These were basic political questions that had to be decided in a deeply competitive world.

The understanding of history that Fukuyama developed therefore was not merely about geopolitical or even party-political competition, but competition over fundamental principles of organizing social life. What made, say, the nuclear arms race world-historic was not merely the awesome destructive capacity or the geopolitical rivalry involved but that it was the armed expression of a contest over the best means of organizing human life.

It is this notion of History that is at stake in these debates – history as a process of institutionalizing different types of collective life, organized around different ways and means of embedding human participation in their own societies. Allied to this claim was the notion that universal patterns of order-formation are discernible and meaningful in the historic process, even if they arise independently of the will of any specific protagonist. For Fukuyama, these participatory structures and recognition of individual needs were exhausted by Western liberal democracy. Thus, to say that the US had won was not simply to vindicate one pole in the bipolar competition of the Cold War era, but to point out that the American victory was global in scope, and epic in historical terms – its implications would be felt everywhere, and it would retrospectively alter the understanding of the sequence of events that led to 1992. If these questions were assumed to be settled and if the formula for human government had been resolved at the core of the international system, then this necessarily had consequences for the structure of government and collective decision-making everywhere.

Fukuyama's grandiose and bold thesis drew plenty of ire, much of it on the basis of misunderstanding. People interpreted Fukuyama wrongly, as if he had claimed that the clocks had stopped, or that nothing would ever happen again, or even that he had endorsed the US specifically over other Western countries. Fukuyama's claim was more basic: not that there would be no more novelty – artificial intelligence, new cities, gene editing – but rather that there would be no fundamental improvement or change to the deep blueprints of politics and social structure. Fukuyama's own sympathies were more social democratic than free market – it is Denmark's welfarist capitalism that fascinates him more than the US[3] – but this does not alter the status of his basic claim. While there might be variation in tax rates and levels of public spending between, say, Denmark and the US, not to mention all sorts of different institutions and practices, the fundamental structures were essentially the same: liberal democracy and liberal market capitalism.

Fukuyama went beyond the hubristic flourish of his original thesis in a book published on the same topic a few years later.[4] In more measured vein, he made clear that the End of History would be enervating and not energizing. Without grand competition over political principles, Fukuyama reasoned that privatized consumerism, hedonism and even nihilism would prevail as dominant sentiments. All the supposed challenges to the End of History thesis – say, new ideologies of the post-Cold War world such as Islamist jihadism and environmentalism – vindicated Fukuyama's central claim. The spread of these ideologies after the end of the US-Soviet clash only ended up exemplifying different aspects – consumerist or nihilist – of the post-historic condition identified by Fukuyama. However murderous and ostentatiously gory it was, jihadism, for instance, was never able to establish any stable pole of opposition or durable model of political order and stability. Whatever mass appeal jihadism and Islamism enjoyed was based on their capacity to strike blows against the American empire, not to replace it, which they were patently incapable of doing.

However resilient autocratic states proved, Fukuyama pointed out that those authoritarian governments that survived waves of post-Cold War democratization nonetheless paid homage to liberal democracy, as was evident in their continuous rigmarole of staging fake elections. Similarly, the new problems that seemed to emanate from the developing world were no longer anti-imperial revolution – that is to say, the creation of new political orders – but rather state collapse and failure. This reaffirmed Fukuyama's basic point: there might be problems to be managed, but there was no alternative to the status quo, no legitimate or viable means of restructuring social and political life for the better – the better had already been achieved.

If the basic formula of human government had been settled, then clearly the range of political variation was more limited by default. This was distinctly visible in domestic political systems around the world: the ideological spectrum of party-political competition was compressed. As the far-left end of the spectrum was snapped off, the far-right range of the spectrum became equally redundant. The political options of the center expanded by default to occupy the entirety of the political spectrum. At the same time, the range of valid policy options shrank as political diversity was reduced. Political parties began to compete more intensively for the center ground, confident that they could keep their older loyalist voting blocs that were anchored in parts of the political spectrum that no longer existed – Paris's "red belt" of working-class districts that had once voted for the Communist

Party, or the Labour Party's ex-industrial heartlands in northern England and the Welsh valleys. "They have nowhere else to go," observed Peter Mandelson, a political strategist of New Labour, an archetypal party of the post-historic era.[5]

Few political scientists or strategists would care or know much about ethereal Hegelian theorizing, nor would they see its relevance to the cut and thrust of party-political competition in the post-Cold War era. Yet the whole process of politics and political science followed in this Hegelian groove. The shrinking ideological space that in turn intensified electoral competition for the center ground gave political life a stability in most developed countries that lent itself to polling, bold generalizations and predictive claims developed using econometric techniques. These trends in turn reinforced the drift toward technocracy and the rule of experts that was already implicit in a post-historic landscape. For if politics was less contested, what need is there for politicians to offer competing visions of society and to try to win over voters? If there is essentially a single template and a limited range of options in applying it, then the issue becomes less one of creativity or of making people's hopes and aspirations actual, than of effective application of that single template – in this case, liberal market capitalism. To govern this single model, what is required is merely expertise, and so political elites made increasing recourse to it. This laid the ground for technocratic rule to become increasingly legitimate, as opposed to the authority of democratic election and representing the will of voters. Centrist neoliberal technocracy became, in short, the model of the moment.

If there are fewer options from which to choose, due to the lack of any fundamental or principled contestation of politics, there is less need to win assent or even extract consent – less need, in sum, to build political support for one particular choice over another. For what need to win support if our choices are self-evident and indisputable? Extend the market, protect human rights. Moreover, institutions built around supposedly self-evident principles of government require no political legitimacy, as they endure no political contestation. The International Monetary Fund, the EU, the World Bank or UN Security Council – or even in the final instance, globalization itself – effectively tells us what to do.

2.1 The beginning of the end of the end...

The era of neoliberal technocracy began to break down in 2008 with the onset of the Global Financial Crisis, as the world's financial circulatory system began to seize up in response to the crumbling of the US sub-prime mortgage market.[6] Vast sums were spent to ensure global liquidity could be maintained in order to keep the global economy stable, although in the end it was the enormous fiscal effort of the Chinese state that helped tug the global economy out of the pit. This was largely because the Chinese state retained capacity in a way that other states didn't, with industrial policy, monetary policy and fiscal policy all concentrated in the hands of the government in Beijing. This allowed it to mount a coordinated recovery. If Beijing demonstrated its effectiveness and Washington had no equivalent industrial policy and no political will to use its fiscal policy – choosing to bail out Wall Street in preference to Main Street – the European Union was at the opposite end of the spectrum to the Chinese state. The EU endured not only the rigidity and brittleness of a currency union without a fiscal union, but industrial policy was also anathema to the EU in its continental attempt to build an integrated, seamless market of smooth competition. Industrial power was overwhelmingly concentrated in Germany, at the expense of other countries, notably Italy. Fiscal policy was crimped by the rules needed to coordinate a single currency out of so many diverse national economies. Thus while the US and China recovered reasonably quickly in terms of the nominal figures of economic growth,

Europe remained mired in crisis. As the debt of the insolvent banks was absorbed by states, the crisis mutated into a sovereign debt crisis.

Austerity became the norm at the state level in the US and at the national level in the EU. All of this exacerbated underlying social ills that had been festering for some time – declining public investment, crumbling infrastructure, vast regional disparities between exurban and peri-urban rings around the urban cores of global financial hubs, which were increasingly concentrated into citadels of wealth and privilege. Wage stagnation, which had been disguised by imports of cheap white goods and electronics from East Asia and policies of easy credit, became increasingly glaring. Property prices that had locked socially aspirant middle- and lower-middle-class Millennials out of the hipster quarters of city centers continued to rise, under the effects of central banks' quantitative easing operations, whose effects inflated asset prices, strengthening those who already owned property and investments. All these factors constituted the streams trickling through the dam of neoliberal technocracy that would eventually burst.

Unsurprisingly, then, the most dramatic political repercussions of the crisis erupted in Europe – the movement of the squares in Spain and Greece, as the debt crisis took its toll on the more debt-prone economies of the southern tier of the Eurozone. Insurgent left parties were formed that sought to harness the popular energy of the squares, finally sweeping into government in Greece in 2015, while the Podemos party formed to the left of the social democrats in Spain. In Britain, a traditional backbench rebel, Jeremy Corbyn, unexpectedly shattered centrist domination of the Labour Party to become the party's leader.

On the other side of the Atlantic and at the other end of the political spectrum, Donald Trump would lead another insurgency within his own Republican Party, shredding the neoliberal domination of the incumbents, substituting his own brand of populism in its place – a vision that even drew the epithet of being "socialist" from one of Trump's rivals in the Republican Party, Ted Cruz. In short, it took the better part of a decade for the structures of centrist hegemony to crumble, as the political results of the 2008 crash became visible the following decade. Although vastly different in obvious ways, from their political outlooks to their personal demeanors, both Trump and Corbyn expressed different manifestations of the crumbling of the neoliberal era – different manifestations of the End of the End of History. Corbyn's unassuming demeanor and long personal history of rebellion on the left of the party gave him authenticity and principle, in contrast to the indifferent, bland, elite managerialism that was radiated by Tony Blair and his successors in 10 Downing Street, Gordon Brown and David Cameron. Trump's crudity and callousness were calculated, intended to signal and confirm his outsider status, despite his personal wealth, facilitating his demotic and nationalistic appeals to rust-belt swing voters disillusioned with President Obama's empty promises of "change." The End of the End of History was visible, across the political spectrum.

If the regime that had developed in the post-Cold War, post-historic era was thus characterized by technocratic centrism, market hegemony and liberal globalization, did that mean that its disintegration presaged a new phase of historic struggle? Would we expect to see meaningful political competition in which it was possible to upgrade the fundamental formulas of collective government? By the logic of Fukuyama's own argument, a "return" to History would require battling over the fundamental principles of social organization. If that were visible, then we could perhaps say that History had restarted. This requires evaluating the character of the social and political struggles emerging out of the breakdown of this era. Much of this is done in subsequent chapters. Before doing that, however, we should consider what further insights, if any, we might be able to squeeze from the Hegelian dialectic to understand (post-) historic processes.

While the preceding neoliberal order was clearly breaking down, there was still no fundamental contestation of the underlying principles of social life, from either Left or Right. Trump was widely denounced as a war-mongering fascist, fully expected by many leading luminaries – journalists, political commentators and leading historians – to collapse the institutions of the US republic into his own personal dictatorship and to pivot to an expansionist, racial white nationalism. Yet what is most striking about Trump's tenure is the lack of any significant policy achievement that differs from mainstream Republican Party politics. The only arguable exception here is that Trump has not (yet) launched a new war – one characteristic that favorably differentiates him from his predecessors. For all the Alt-Right's fondness for Trump – so widely visible on social media in 2016 – this too dissolved in the miasma of conventional GOP politics and Trump's cultivation of a much larger electoral base. With the partial exception of rust-belt swing voters, voting and patterns of political conflict in the US have for the most part continued along the Republican-Democratic cleavage.

In France, President Emmanuel Macron's brand of yuppy populism occupies the liberal center that had been the home of the Socialist Party before its disintegration. In Britain, for all of Corbyn's putative radicalism, he could not extend it to countenance a break with Brussels or offer unequivocal support for Britain's withdrawal from the EU – and this despite his own personal history of Euroscepticism. Corbyn's willingness to consider subverting the outcome of the 2016 referendum to withdraw from the EU shattered the Labour Party's electoral coalition of working- and middle-class voters, with the former more strongly in favor of leaving the EU and the latter in favor of staying. In Greece, similarly, the Syriza government that had initially been hailed everywhere as the first radical government ever to be elected into office in Europe, perpetuated austerity policies and refused to withdraw Greece from the Eurozone – this after having led a referendum revolt on the terms of another EU bailout.

The point of these examples – there are plenty of others that could serve just as well – is to illustrate that although the party systems, ideologies and personalities seemed to have changed, there was little challenge to underlying institutions, principles or structures. The implosion of the French socialists – a party that traces its heritage all the way back to Jean Jaurès and the Second International itself – was the consummation of a long process of neoliberalization of that party; it made itself redundant before it was wiped out by Macron.[7] Indeed, perhaps the single most dramatic and lasting political change that breaks with previous patterns is the loss of the British Labour Party's northern English working-class base. That some of these voters have been captured by Britain's Tory party ensures that even this most significant of electoral disruptions will broadly fall into a familiar pattern of British politics; that is to say, a rejuvenated pre-Thatcherite One-Nation Toryism that combines the Tory's middle-class and capitalist support with that of the working class.

In other words, despite the disintegration of a whole political order, what is replacing it does not significantly alter underlying patterns of politics. Insofar as there are significant and visible changes – for example, the regional fragmentation of the global economy, the uncoupling of Sino-US economic interdependence, the disintegration of the much-vaunted just-in-time supply chains across borders – these are all spontaneous processes, propelled by the over-reach and fragility of global capitalism. These are changes that, although accelerated by the response to a viral pandemic, are not the inauguration of anyone's new ideology or political program. The novel coronavirus has no agenda, no manifesto, no plan – the entropy that it has produced exposes the underlying frailty of neoliberal capitalism, and the striking degree of state failure that is visible in so many governments' responses to the pandemic indicates drift, not mastery, of the historic process. The profound lack of capacity of major industrialized nations effectively to respond to Covid-19 – with hollowed-out industrial sectors, no industrial policies, deep inequalities, flexible labor markets collapsing like dominoes – exemplified the fact that the precipitous changes prompted by responses to the virus did not indicate any attempt by political actors to shape or control the direction of events.

Thus, if it is clear that the End of History has ended, it is likewise evident that History has not restarted; what we are witnessing is further fragmentation, disintegration and drift. Fukuyama's own picture did not account for the fact that the order he described might crumble away. Meanwhile, none of his various efforts to modulate or restructure his thesis – to incorporate new populisms and new forms of identity politics – fully convince. We also know that we have been here before. This is not the first end of the End of History.

2.2 Deaths foretold

Already, in the aftermath of the Al Qaeda terror attacks on the Pentagon and New York in 2001, the US neoconservative Fareed Zakaria proclaimed the End of the End of History, by which he meant the end of the supposed ease and comfort of the post-Cold War era that had been secured by the prosperity of global growth.[8] Zakaria expected this era, by necessity, to give way to the curtailing of democratic liberties and a new twilight struggle that would rely on covert operations and proxy forces, much like the Cold War itself. Neoconservative Robert Kagan and strategic theorist Azar Gat saw the return of history in the growth of geopolitical rivalry between the West on the one hand, and Russia and China on the other.[9]

Indeed, even in the midst of the Cold War itself, there were some who thought that history had been transcended. The years after the Second World War and before the tumult of the 1960s were also melancholically announced as the "end of ideology" by the likes of Daniel Bell and others – with rising living standards, stable mixed economies and convergence among industrialized nations around large states with powerful bureaucracies independent of nominal ideological commitments.[10] The Soviet premier Nikita Khrushchev's secret speech in 1956 denouncing his predecessor Stalin not only seemed to vindicate Western liberal capitalism but also seemed to offer the prospect of liberalization, reform and democratization in the Soviet bloc, as well as détente in the Cold War. As we have seen, Fukuyama himself was inspired by Kojève, who took global superpower condominium and postwar European integration itself as the End of History.

Perhaps, though, the end of our early twenty-first century End of History regime is more thoroughgoing than the closure of Kojève's 1950s End of History, or the 2001 version, not least because the *ancien régime* of globalist liberalism is being eroded within the Western world itself (and not through confrontation with ragtag Islamist militias in remote and peripheral regions of the world). Given the varieties of histories and ends-of-histories embedded in these conflicting views, it is worth briefly revisiting the original idea of History as developed by Hegel himself.

If we examine Hegel's own picture a little more closely, things appear more complicated.[11] Hegel himself, of course, progenitor of the original thesis, never claimed that History had ended in 1815 or that the clocks had stopped, any more than Fukuyama had in 1989. The notion of the End of History was built into the structure of Hegel's whole philosophical system, which was explicitly historicized – that is to say, its notions and concepts were cast in historical terms of development and change, with the implication that his own insights were necessarily the culmination of a long prior historical process. We should dwell a little on the context and rationale of Hegel's thought. Unlike the American political scientist Fukuyama, Hegel's views were inspired by defeat, not victory – and a double defeat at that, the first being Napoleon's dissolution of the Holy Roman Empire in 1804, followed by Napoleon's own ultimate defeat and downfall in 1815. Napoleon's annexation and domination of the German states that had previously constituted the Empire did not sadden Hegel, however, despite his being German. Indeed, he was famously awed to see Napoleon riding his horse on a reconnaissance mission when Hegel's own city of Jena was occupied by French troops, causing dramatic personal disruption to Hegel's own life and career.

The reason that Hegel supported Napoleon was that he saw Napoleon as universalizing the benefits of constitutionally ordered, secular nationhood and political independence across Europe. Hegel welcomed these developments, even if they came at the expense of French domination of Germany. Hegel was invested in a higher principle than the relative standing of the Germanic world in relation to France. At a deeper level, beyond the passing humiliation and subordination of the German states at the hands of Napoleon, Hegel's project was to salvage the historic gains of the French Revolution – not only in the reordering of the German states undertaken by Napoleon, but also beyond the post-Napoleonic settlement itself, established at the Congress of Vienna in 1815 after Napoleon's final defeat and downfall. The fruits of this effort were the philosophical schema of the constitutional state presented in Hegel's *Philosophy of Right*, in which the gains of individual freedom were embedded in social and political institutions. Perhaps there was even a third and more important defeat for Hegel's historic vision and one that mattered more to Hegel himself. On the eve of his death in the plague year of 1831, he was troubled by the news from Paris of another revolution that overthrew the legitimist Bourbon monarch Charles X – a development that suggested that there was a deeper turbulence within the post-Napoleonic world than Hegel had anticipated.

That Hegel was thinking through the consequences of the defeat and mangling of the French Revolution, rather than an imperial victory as Fukuyama was, is significant. Hegel's view of the End of History was not, in fact, bound up with any specific form of the post-Napoleonic settlement in Europe – indeed, it was not attached to the design or functioning of any specific political structure or order. We know this because Hegel optimistically looked across the ocean to the Americas as opening up new vistas for humanity that made Europe seem like an "old lumber room" by comparison. Hegel's claim about the End of History did not rest on the durability and stasis of the post-Napoleonic settlement, but rather on the irreversible character of certain historic developments with respect to our collective self-understanding. Most important of these was the universality of *freedom* within the modern world that had been unleashed by the French Revolution. In Hegel's view, the specific historic gain of the French Revolution was to reveal the universal character of human freedom, that is, the claim that freedom is in fact part of being human. Freedom was thus not merely an abstract philosophical proposition, but a political proposition that could be realized in concrete institutions. This was Hegel's original meaning of the End of History – that whatever followed the French Revolution had to be based on the universal claims of human freedom. This in turn meant that no social or political order could ever be fully stable. The significance of this insight is that freedom cannot be limited or appended to one specific regime or order, as it is precisely the expansiveness and restlessness of human freedom that exceeds any one specific set of political and social institutions.

It is this that explains how there can be a finality to the historic process – after the French Revolution, the irreversible and simultaneously contradictory character of human freedom serves as a backstop to history. The Franco-American revolutions of the eighteenth and nineteenth centuries meant that successful political orders would subsequently, necessarily, have to be built on universal claims that seek to incorporate the demands of human freedom. At the same time, there will also be recurrent ends-of-the-end-of-history. We know that any regime in the modern era that does not embed human freedom in its collective life will be limited and partial; likewise we know that human freedom cannot be exhausted by any specific set of institutions and structures. That the End of History would recur – and that the End of the End of History would also recur – would be entirely consistent with Hegel's own idea that freedom would necessarily spill over the boundaries of any concrete political order. How far this dissatisfaction with any specific regime can be converted into a conscious grasp and manipulation of the historic process is a separate question. Hegel's real insight is that no order founded on human freedom can be ossified; all ends of history end, all modern political orders are eventually remade.

It is this understanding that helps explain the limited character of left-populist attempts to break through the impasse of our most recent end of the end of history. In their failure to overturn neoliberalism, left-populism failed to expand the meaning of what was politically possible – left-populists did not manage to expand people's political control over their own lives and societies because they did not key into the agency of their own citizens.

Properly understood then, the End of History and the End of the End of History should be no surprise, or at least not a surprise to those who understand the original terms of the theory. By the same token, that a particular political order corrodes from within is no guarantee that we have restarted contesting the fundamental organizing principles of collective life either. For, if anything is apparent from Hegel, it is that the latter requires not only a comprehensive vision of universal emancipation, but also the political willingness to substitute it for the status quo. And that necessitates the willingness to tolerate the inevitable disruption that follows, as the structures and institutions of the *ancien régime* are broken up.

Chapter 3

The Danger of Democracy: From Post-Politics to Anti-Politics

Under the political arrangements of neoliberal democracy, held as the model for the world, change should have been constant. Indeed, "change" was a major component of the official ideology of the time. Tolerance of disruption to the status quo should have been built in. After all, liberalism holds that autonomous individuals are free to pursue their ends, limited only to the extent those ends impede the autonomy of others. Governments, in a democracy, are accountable to the interests and desires of citizens. Society, therefore, is dynamic; politics should naturally respond, with representative mechanisms working to channel social demands upwards.

That is the official story. In practice, during the End of History period political change was foreclosed, prevented from ever really being on the agenda. But this "post-political" means of preventing contestation could only last so long, it could only temporarily repress popular passions while debt-fueled consumption assuaged anxieties. Once these means were exhausted, the upholders of the liberal-democratic order were made to face a waking nightmare. In the 1990s and 2000s rejection of political establishments – *anti-politics* – was sporadic; by the mid-2010s, this force came to eclipse the reigning post-politics. Elites called it "populism" – "the greatest danger to the contemporary West."[1] It is the illegitimate, rejected child of the current political order. To some, it was even a threat to order itself. And it is such a large, expansive threat, so all-embracing, that the evils named "populism" outnumber all other forces.

3.1 We're all populists now

Historical populism – etymologically linked to "the people" and therefore to "popular" – included everything from its originators in the nineteenth century – the People's Party in the US and the Narodinks in Russia – to Poujadism in France, Nasserism in Egypt and Peronism in Argentina. More recently, it has included the likes of Silvio Berlusconi, Hugo Chavez, Geert Wilders, Occupy or even Viktor Orban. One is tempted to conclude that the object of "populism" is so vague as to say more about those who use it than those about whom it is used.

And what purpose does this serve? "Populism" functions to link disparate movements of Left and Right, to recast any and every political force proposing a national alternative to globalization and the age of "there is no alternative" as two sides of the same coin. So-called populists, in the eyes of responsible administrators of the liberal order, are also authoritarian. In a further leap, the identification of "populist" with "popular" seems to suggest populism is not just the creation of unscrupulous political entrepreneurs, but rather an outgrowth of the people's innate desire for despotism,[2] the irrational furies of the mob.

According to this description, populists would be countered by a sane, evidence-based and liberal anti-populist "center," holding strong against the tide. The Covid-19 crisis brought this dimension into focus, as the health emergency saw chief medical officers take center-stage, to the relief of anti-populists. Evidence-based lockdowns were heralded, while "populist" figures like Brazilian president Jair Bolsonaro or US president Donald Trump were admonished for irrationally downplaying the matter.[3]

The reality, though, is that what counts as "centrism" and what is deemed "populism" is in the eye of the beholder. Moreover, it was the former that laid the ground for the latter. In order to shine a light on this seeming paradox, we should remind ourselves of the stories of two exemplary figures of centrism – former US president Bill Clinton and former British prime minister Tony Blair. Both took power after more than a decade of the neoliberal New Right breaking up the old social-democratic arrangements. They promised a more inclusionary as well as a more modern politics, divested of past attachments. Former governor of Arkansas Bill Clinton won the Democratic Party's nomination in 1992, aiming to push the party toward the political center (that is, rightwards). He adopted the term "vital center" to characterize his politics. This earned a rebuke from Arthur Schlesinger, in some ways the official historian of American liberalism, who coined the term in 1949. Schlesinger had conceived of the vital center as a means of describing liberal democracy itself, in contrast to socialism and fascism. Clinton, in his perversion of the term, was claiming that the center was a narrow combination of neoliberal policies. In so doing, he was positioning the center "closer to Ronald Reagan than Franklin D. Roosevelt," as Schlesinger put it.[4] But more than just shifting the center rightwards, Clinton was narrowing the boundaries of the politically acceptable, beyond which everything else would be "extreme." He was, in doing so, foreclosing political contestation.

Here was the return of the "horseshoe theory," a concept that was conceived during the Cold War to portray fascism and communism as identical. The idea was that the further you stray from the political center, the more the extremes come to resemble one another. Both extremes were "totalitarian"; Stalin and Hitler held hands. But in Clinton's version, the points had so narrowed as to better be seen as hairpin theory. The only legitimate political ground was this narrow stretch of grass. Even social democracy was now a bog, as was traditional conservatism, with its outmoded racism and sexism.

Our second exemplary figure is Tony Blair. In the lead-up to the 2019 UK General Election, the former PM characterized both Labour and Conservative proposals for higher public spending, as well as their resistance to reversing Brexit, as "populism running riot": "Around the world, where political leaders are gathered, there is often a conversation about whose politics is crazier...I agree that right now the competition is fierce. But I still believe British politics is unfortunately ahead of the pack."[5] Blair consequently imagined (wrongly) that a majority of British citizens held a "desire, bordering on the febrile, to end the mess, to wake from the nightmare." The nightmare – the ending of the End of History – required a liberal, anti-populist savior. Some scholars have attempted to give populism a more concrete definition, beyond the dark fantasies of yesterday's men like Tony Blair – surely the real "left behind." Cas Mudde, one of the most cited scholars on the question, sees populism as an ideology that casts society as being separated into two homogenous and antagonistic groups, the pure people versus the corrupt elite. Politics, accordingly, should be an expression of the "general will," allowing little ground for pluralism.[6] Alternatively, when it is not a fully-fledged ideology, it is at least a discursive style: "politics for ordinary people by extraordinary leaders who construct ordinary profiles," as it has been snappily put.[7] For Mudde, populists are ultimately moralistic rather than programmatic.

Here, though, we encounter a complication. This now-standard definition only invites confusion. Tony Blair, when in opposition, railed against "Tory sleaze." Upon taking office in 1997, he promised to be "purer than pure," unlike the corrupt Conservative establishment. He projected a very personalized image of youth, modernity and ethics. "We are the servants now," he declared, pledging to "restore trust in politics." Look what is presented here: a moralistic register, a corrupt elite, personalistic politics with leaders parading as ordinary... the full populist gamut. Or take the example of the other key centrist, Bill Clinton, who, in his saxophone-playing folksiness and I-feel-your-pain emoting, leaned heavily on the concept of the "American heartland," even coining the term "heartland citizens."

Even these exemplars and architects of the Third Way, of neoliberal technocracy and "beyond left and right," could be labeled populists. It is for this reason that contemporary populism should be understood as a child of the current political order. Populism was birthed by the End of History and, at the End of the End of History, came to dethrone post-politics.

Anti-populists, meanwhile, are defined only by their own defensiveness. They cry about threats to liberalism or democracy or liberal democracy, ignoring the multitude of ways they have themselves undermined democratic politics. Anti-populists cast anything that appeals to the people as "populist" – and therefore irresponsible. Culpability for this state of affairs rests with those unscrupulous politicians who think it is okay to respond to the people's irresponsible demands, instead of following expert advice. The very act of being popular seems to be under question. This is losers' logic, the standpoint of those who have been left behind by history.

3.2 The "regular guy"

But what are the people's "demands" today? Demands made of politicians seem above all to voice mistrust – of politicians themselves and of political institutions. Research examining citizens' attitudes to politics and politicians over time has found contrasting folk theories as to what the "good politician" should be, from the mid-twentieth century and the early twenty-first century.[8] While a desire for politicians who are trustworthy, strong, capable and inspiring are perennial, what is new is an emphasis on politicians who are "normal" and "in touch." The distance between politics and the people, state and society, has grown to such an extent that politicians belong to a class apart, different in habits, behavior and appearance, whose concerns are removed from those of ordinary citizens.[9]

The authors of the aforementioned study attribute this change to three factors: the professionalization of politics, such that politicians seem to form a separate, homogenous class; the ideology of intimacy, leading citizens to expect warmth and authenticity from interactions with politicians; and democratic egalitarianism, which has encouraged people to identify the "common" with the right or the good. These arguments would seem to reflect the social critic Christopher Lasch's arguments about the culture of narcissism, whereby emotionalism overwhelms public life. For Lasch, democracy "has come to serve simply as a description of the therapeutic state. When we speak of democracy today, we refer, more often than not, to the democratization of 'self-esteem.' The current catchwords – diversity, compassion, empowerment, entitlement – express the wistful hope that deep divisions in American society can be bridged by goodwill and sanitized speech."[10]

So, today's hostility to politics is premised on significant changes to our conceptions of public and private. Politicians vaunt their personal attributes and seek to portray themselves as everymen; meanwhile we expect politics to care about our feelings. Over the course of the 1990s and 2000s, politicians played a double game: on the one hand they sold themselves as competent technical administrators, on the other, they tried to earn citizens' trust by appealing to everyday values. Bill Clinton's claim to "feel your pain" is an obvious example, but the true master of this art was Silvio Berlusconi, who flaunted his everyday desires and prejudices in an effort to connect – which he did with some success (see Chapter 6). This is "lifestyle politics," in which the boundaries between formal politics and everyday life are broken down. Politics becomes spectacle, in which the Houses of Government and the Big Brother House come to resemble each other; both are stages.

Today, Blairism and Clintonism have been roundly rejected; Berlusconi's charm has also worn off. These politicians are denounced as phonies, standard-bearers of detested machine politics and the priority of image over substance. The same kind of lifestyle politics no longer sells, as mistrust of politics has ascended to new heights. The distance between politics and people can no longer be smoothed over by a "guy you'd want to have a beer with" (as George W Bush was notoriously cast). Even Donald Trump, though he still avails himself of lifestyle politics, would not have succeeded without a more forceful rejection of the political status quo.

Populism is therefore best understood as one example of *anti-politics*. Populists proclaim the bankruptcy of institutions – as when Trump famously referred to Washington DC as a swamp – and denounce the mainstream media as biased, elections as rigged and polls as untrustworthy. They give voice to an open secret: the emperor has no clothes, the credibility of the establishment has disintegrated. In no longer accepting the old politics of consensus, populists and the popular alienation to which they respond are potentially politicizing. As one journalistic account of anti-politics has it, populism is "simultaneously an anti-political movement and an expression of desire for the return of politics proper."[11]

3.3 The dialect, and dialectic, of anti-politics

Though it attracts less fearmongering than populism, "anti-politics" does increasingly draw consternation and confusion. The short-lived but historically profligate presidential campaign of billionaire Michael Bloomberg in 2020, *The Spectator* warned, may fall foul of anti-politics; one of the legions of centrist *Guardian* columnists, Rafael Behr, insists "we need better politicians, not anti-politics"; and even the Marxist literary theorist Terry Eagleton slates anarchism for being anti-political. Indeed, the *New Statesman* points out that the anti-politics preached by then-UKIP MEP Robert Kilroy-Silk in the 2000s "is everywhere" now. But does anyone challenging the establishment count as an anti-politician? As one young British woman active in grassroots organizing told a journalist, "All these experts say that people are 'anti-politics' right now, but what we're seeing [new, insurgent movements] is the epitome of politics."[12] A confusing picture indeed.

There were rumblings of a growing anti-politics earlier on, with dotted references found in the 2000s, such as when *The Sunday Tribune* characterized the 2000 May Day protests as "anti-politics voting with its feet" against globalization. *The Irish Independent* warned in 2008 that Silvio Berlusconi both benefited from and was threatened by "anti-politics." And on a BBC Radio 4 program, a Sciences Po professor noted that, since 63 percent of French people had abandoned notions of Left and Right, they had thereby "politicized anti-politics."[13] The seeds were already being sown.

Yet, prior to the Global Financial Crisis of 2008, the overriding concern among the political class, in their relation to citizens, was voter apathy. *How do we get citizens to care?* Now, however, citizens are angry and unruly; the political class' authority has evaporated entirely. And it is global: in many places, the legitimacy of politics itself is under challenge, from Brexit to the Gilets Jaunes, Brazil to Bulgaria.

The challenge comes from "outside"; the political class – or the establishment, the oligarchy, the political elite, *la casta* in Spain or Italy – are "inside" the system. Political entrepreneurs try to mobilize anger against those on the inside. But when those populist outsiders challenge the political class, the standard response on the Left is to point out that they are not true outsiders, that they do not challenge *economic* interests. True; but we must understand why it is that *political* elites have most often ended up targets of popular ire, and why the only major political breakthroughs of the past decade have tended to come from "populists" – that is, those who are or pose as outsiders – and not the traditional Left, who (ostensibly) represent an economic relation, those "below" against those "above."

In fact, populism seems to muddy distinctions of Left and Right; many populist politicians are ideologically ambivalent figures. In this, the insurgent populists are mirror images of the incumbent managerialists, who also disavowed ideology. Rule by the latter over the past 3 decades succeeded in depoliticizing the economy. With the economy naturalized, formal "left vs right" politics lost its meaning, or transformed into a culture war rather than a struggle for power. Now, in our anti-political age, political antagonism returns to the scene in a new form: "outsiders vs insiders." But there is a trap: the widespread mistrust of political leaders afflicts not just establishment politicians, but can also corrode the authority of any movement – including the people's trust in its own capacity to take power.

Politics, in its essence, is division, a disruption of the normal way of doing things, the fundamental presumption of equality, such that anyone could claim political authority. In this sense, *anti-politics can be politicizing.* But politics is also about representation: the funneling of popular interests, desires and dreams to agents endowed with the responsibility to translate that will into action. That responsibility, then, is a question of political authority: the legitimate use of coercion, without which any militancy for a better future will fold. In this sense, *anti-politics can be de-politicizing.* If democratic political authority cannot be established, anti-democratic forms will succeed. So unless we wish politics to be nothing other than authoritarian measures exercised over cowed masses, politicizing the present is the only way to wedge open the future.

In accordance with the understanding that anti-politics can be either politicizing or depoliticizing, it is important to operate with a definition of politics that avoids narrow identification with "formal politics," or the specific manifestation of liberal democracy. This would be something like seeing politics as a democratic urge, one that can appear in different times and places. By using this sort of definition we can also avoid golden ageism – a principal failing of most writing on depoliticization – whereby the Cold War period is held as the ideal model to be recreated.

3.4 Smothering politics at the End of History

To understand how populism expresses anti-politics, while simultaneously expressing a desire for politicization, we have to understand what *post-politics* was: a strategy of de-politicization.

Post-politics is a form of government that tries to foreclose political contestation by emphasizing consensus, eradicating ideology and ruling through managerial technocracy. In other words, it is the assertion that all important questions are settled, so all that remains for political discussion are questions of technical implementation. During the End of History, politicians thrust citizens into a double bind. As the ideological spectrum was narrowed, people lost interest and became increasingly disengaged. Sensing this withdrawal of assent and waning legitimacy, politicians would go begging to citizens. Electoral participation was cast as a good in itself. "Vote or die," for instance, was a popular slogan in the build-up to the 2004 elections in the United States. Various technical innovations were proffered, such as lowering the voting age, devolving power to regions, or other means of encouraging participatory decision-making. But this response was based on error. Depoliticization does not emanate from citizens' consciousness; the origin of the matter is not "voter apathy."

Depoliticization is in fact a political strategy, which takes place at the levels of institutions and processes. The practice of governing became insulated from popular pressures, with the classic example being the independence granted to central banks, which removed monetary policy from the realm of politics. So, how interest rates are set, and thus the consequent balance between employment rates, prices and economic growth, is removed from public contestation. Decisions about monetary policy become consequent upon central bankers' evaluations – or, more pointedly, what they understand to be in the interests of "the economy," itself code for "business interests." In doing so, collective problems are turned into natural consequences of a self-regulating order – the market. Historical contingencies become necessary ones – globalization is not a choice but an objective imposition, requiring pre-determined responses. And popular sovereignty – political power in the hands of the people – is traded off in favor of consumer sovereignty or limited individual liberty.[14] In other words, the possibility of exercising democratic control over key institutions is foreclosed.

Any challenge to this order is treated as an angry throwback, attributed to malcontents motivated by irrational desires. At the extreme, these are classed as macho, misogynist, homophobic or racist – the ultimate crimes against pluralistic, consensus politics – whether true or not. The Brexit slogan "take back control" was dismissed as mere cover for xenophobia, ignoring the democratic deficit to which it responded. Supporters of Bernie Sanders were ridiculed as "bros," as if the redistributive policies he advocated could only be of interest to young white men. By slanderous means, any popular demand is treated as illegitimate, and formal politics ceases to be an avenue for real political contestation.

A concept adjacent to "post-politics" is what the political scientist Colin Crouch calls "post-democracy." This is a society that still retains the formal institutions of democracy (parties, elections, parliaments) but in which these are increasingly empty shells, divested of popular energies and innovation. To illustrate: election after election features catch-all parties trying to capture the center ground – middle-class "swing voters" – while purveying near-identical policies; class divisions are denied; and decision-making becomes the purview of political elites in less- or non-representative arenas (such as the office of the executive, quangos, the now-independent central bank, etc.). What emerges is a growing entanglement between public and private sectors, with economic elites increasingly able to influence matters by circumventing representative bodies. For Crouch, post-democracy is a situation in which politicians still need citizens' assent, obtained through elections, but a voter's position is that of a manipulated object, rather than a self-conscious subject. *Post*-democracy can be contrasted with *pre*-democratic and with *democratic* regimes. In pre-democratic arrangements, elites would flaunt their class privilege and demand acknowledgment of subordination from the lower orders. Democracy proper allows for the challenging of these acknowledged hierarchies. Post-democracy is unique in denying the very existence of privatization and subordination.[15] "We are all middle-class now," as former deputy prime minister to Tony Blair, John Prescott, famously trumpeted in 1997.

The populist irruptions across the West, then, are challenges to this state of affairs. They are angry responses to not being listened to. One of the things that marks the transition from the End of History to the End of the End of History is the difference in responses to depoliticization. Whereas an apathetic disengagement from post-politics was the predominant disposition in the 1990s and 2000s, an angry anti-political rejection of politics marks the 2010s and 2020s.

Political theory has largely not grasped this development, concerned as it is with questions internal to "politics." It is not in the habit of perceiving politics from the outside, as a category. But the advent of post-politics and the response it has provoked – anti-politics – asks questions of us: What is politics, and what is good or bad about it? And consequently, what is anti-politics? And if anti-politics is bad, what is bad about it? Put differently, how do we tread the line between two dangers? In one, we make the error of identifying politics *as such* with the existing political order, the status quo, the compromises of liberal democracy; in the other, we fall into a rejectionist position, in which politicians, elections, parties – even democracy in its essence – are understood to be a sham.

3.5 If that was post-politics, what is politics?

One way out of this Gordian Knot is to reconceive all political philosophies – ideas about how politics should work – as pushing toward the end of politics.[16] Instead of linking "politics" to the exercise of power or to specific institutions (parliaments, elections, etc.), we should see it as a *dynamic,* one which upends the normal way of doing things. But this presents a paradox: when you achieve your political aims, politics ends. Consider liberalism: according to this philosophy, the ideal is an orderly process by which plural social interests are represented at the political level. Everyone agrees to the rules of the game: a regular alternation of power occurs, along with the essential institutional checks and balances guaranteeing a just order. Private individuals can go about their business safe in the knowledge that the administration of society is being carried out in a peaceful and equitable manner. Harmony is achieved, ergo, politics is eliminated.

Or take any other of the main political-ideological traditions – conservatism, socialism or fascism. An authentic conservative dream envisions political action submitted to a greater authority, say, the Church, which ordains the proper place of every group and stratum. Politics is limited to its minimum necessary action: the maintenance of this traditional order. The space for politics is almost non-existent. In socialist thought, revolution would overthrow the bourgeois order and its competing groups (classes). If politics is the product of scarcity, of the struggle over the distribution of the social product, then the end of scarcity under communism would see the end of politics as such. Or, finally, consider the heightened class struggle of the interwar period, a historical peak of politicization, which was resolved through the smashing of the workers' movement through extra-parliamentary, paramilitary means. The politics of fascism, too, aims at the end of politics.

If we think of politics as a dynamic, as the upending of hierarchies, then a lot of what normally goes by the name "politics" – the use of power, the practice of government – is most of the time just the policing of order or the administration of people. This understanding restores to politics its link to politicization, the putting of things into question or into dispute. For philosopher Slavoj Zizek, "politics and democracy are synonymous." This he demonstrates by recourse to the example of anti-democratic politics, which "always and by definition is and was depoliticization, i.e. the unconditional demand that 'things should return to normal,' with each individual doing his or her particular job."[17]

Understanding this identity has two important consequences for us today. Firstly, it rips "democracy" from the specific form we usually encounter it, liberal democracy (which is what usually gets defended by proponents of the End of History – see Chapter 2). "Democracy," according to the latter understanding, is a placid society, no longer driven by passion for political honor or heroism; it is an ambient milieu: the natural habitat of postmodern individualism.[18] More darkly, postmodern liberal democracy can be understood according to the terms the late cultural theorist Mark Fisher proposed – "capitalist realism" – in which society is overwhelmed by a depressive mood, only enlivened by fleeting, consumerist moments of hedonism. This is not our understanding of democracy. Democracy is a weapon, not a state. Further, it is the collective shaping of social and political life; it emerges as *popular power*.

Secondly, this identity of politics and democracy should alert us to the dangers of left-wing anti-politics. Democracy is grounded in the presumption of the equality of anyone and everyone. When this encounters the business-as-usual of administration, it creates politics, which demonstrates that politicization is the essential starting point for those seeking an egalitarian order. Politics is the home of the Left, whereas the quelling of political enthusiasm is the natural home of the Right. This stands to reason. Consider the recent historical trajectory: the End of History was initiated by the global defeat of socialism. The post-political order that followed was justified by an ideology that pretended to be non-ideological. It was in effect a mask for the untrammeled rule of capital. Where there is no systemic alternative, there is no politics. Therefore, when the Left falls prey to the logic of anti-politics, it signs its death warrant.

3.6 Abandon dreams of a golden age

What, then, accounts for the sense that, "before, there was politics; then, at the End of History, there was not?" In answering this question, most scholars default to a view that the postwar era in Western Europe was "real politics." But this would be to restrict our conception to the circumscribed parliamentary forms of that period. After all, it is worth remembering that the institutional order back then also sought to lock-in politics, lest it overflow – as it had done in the 1920s and 30s. Many found the postwar period to be depoliticized. Indeed, the New Left in the 1960s rebelled against what it saw as a stultifying, totally administered society. As we already saw, critic Daniel Bell wrote *The End of Ideology* in 1960, on the eve of the New Left's efflorescence. As with the previous ends of history encountered in Chapter 2, the death of politics has been announced before, too.

What is novel, however, about the liberal-democratic End of History is its institution of *post*-politics, an end to politics distinct from pre-democratic feudal conservatism, or the social-democratic tedium of the postwar era. It is a stronger negation, whereby politics is not merely repressed but *foreclosed*. Another way of putting this is that the formal politics of parties, elections, parliament, and so on hardly feature the traces of the social conflict happening in reality (as one-sided as that conflict became). Any challenge to this state of affairs was – and still is – treated as pure irrationality.

Why, then, did the postwar epoch, dominated by the Cold War, seem to produce politics? The answer is to be found in the threat posed to "normal politics" by something beyond: the workers' movement and revolutionary socialist politics domestically and the existence of the Soviet Union abroad. These forces kept national bourgeoisies relatively "honest," allowing space for the democratic game (in Western Europe at least). The real existence of class struggle meant political conflict could not be ignored or cognitively erased. Instead, the response of national political elites was that political conflict should play out within accepted bounds.[19]

The encounter of the threat of revolution, on the one hand, with states founded on a commitment to the rights of man (liberty, equality and fraternity), on the other, created the necessary tension for democracy to flourish. It was, of course, a limited democracy – one made up of set rules and a limited number of acknowledged parties. But electoral and civic participation was high, there were mass parties, trade unions represented the working man, and there were means of transmitting popular interests upwards to the state. Crouch terms this historical trajectory the "parabola of democracy," which accompanied the "parabola of working-class politics": democracy accompanied the growth, strength, organization and self-assurance of the working class, reaching its peak "around the mid-point of the twentieth century," either before or after the Second World War, depending on location.[20] The decline of working-class politics foretells the decline of politics itself.

So, while the postwar period in Western Europe and North America was no golden age, it *was* a more democratic period than today. The historical defeat of the workers movement, and of socialism, ended up extinguishing politics itself. Hence the surprising gloominess in Fukuyama's heralding of the End of History.

3.7 A knock on the door

A striking illustration of the repression of politics at a moment when it threatened to return can be found in the scandal over wildcat strikes that hit the UK energy industry in early 2009 – an early salvo in the End of the End of History. Workers at Total's Lindsey Oil Refinery in Lincolnshire, England were outraged that an Italian construction contractor had hired-in several hundred mainly Italian and Portuguese contractors, undercutting local workers. A 47 percent increase in unemployment in the county over that year – in a region already suffering from deindustrialization dating back decades – combined with the general effects of the Global Financial Crisis created a precarious situation. The placards on the picket line proclaimed "British jobs for British workers" – a response to the EU's Posted Workers Directive, itself a means of undermining workers' rights disguised as the right to free movement in Europe. The BBC portrayed the strikers as xenophobes and racists, while the media as a whole tended to frame debates about the strikes exclusively as "racist: yes or no?"

This was despite protestations from union officials that it was a strike against foreign companies' behavior, not foreigners. Indeed, there were many accounts of workers repulsing attempts by the far-right British National Party to co-opt the strike.[21] Even so, New Labour prime minister Gordon Brown called the strikes "indefensible." The irony was that Brown himself had used the old National Front slogan "British jobs for British workers" only 2 years prior, in a major speech. Moreover, ruling New Labour governments had had no compunction in hamming up "concerns over immigration" when it suited their electoral priorities – and indeed the government maintained strict controls on non-EU migration. Brown defended himself claiming that, when he had used the line in 2007, he "was talking about giving people in Britain the skills so that they have the ability to get jobs which were at present going to people from abroad…" Even a political pygmy like the Conservative leader at the time, David Cameron, recognized the hypocrisy: "On the one hand [Gordon Brown] lectures everyone about globalization and on the other he borrows this slogan from the BNP."[22]

The post-political foreclosure of politics can be seen here in all its stultification: the rules of globalization are set in stone and they work for everyone; if you fail, it is your fault – you should instead compete harder in the market (by acquiring skills); concerns about workers' rights are unfounded and they will be ignored; any expression of dissent can only be the product of dark antediluvian impulses.

Throughout the 1990s and 2000s, events such as these were sporadic and ephemeral enough to be dealt with confidently by political elites. But as the new decade unfolded, the establishment lost its grasp. In 2015, the previously marginal leftist MP Jeremy Corbyn unexpectedly became leader of the Labour Party. Meanwhile, in the US, Donald Trump's candidacy was gaining steam, to the incredulity of nearly all observers. We know what happened the following year in each country, and the reactions to it by the liberal establishment (which are the subject of the next chapter). And the same process was repeating everywhere that the foreclosure of politics had been successful, and against which people were now rebelling. For those whose political and cultural authority was premised on a society emptied of all politics and social conflict, all this suddenly looked like irrationality was winning.

Now, it should be clear that not every revolt against the post-political is worthy of support. Often, these take xenophobic or exclusionary forms, or their anti-politics is a recursive and self-defeating dead-end. But it is important to understand why revolt takes the forms it does in our age. With traditional representatives of the working classes – the social-democratic parties – fully signed up to neoliberal globalization, there are few "respectable" avenues for protesting against economic and cultural degradation, nor political leadership to give voice to these sentiments in the appropriately coded forms of political discourse. Hatred, in the post-political era, is suppressed or invalidated, to the extent that even simple disagreement is pathologized. Dissenting expressions then explode in other venues, often on social media, raw and angry. And the more they are objects of censure, the greater the temptation to poke at elite sensitivities.

Insofar as the "populists" seize the opportunity and adopt these frustrations, giving voice to them in the arena of formal politics, they serve as agents of re-politicization, of thrusting into the realm of closed-doors administration the idea of the equality of anyone and everyone to speak. Indeed, as we've seen, they are essentially defined by the fact that they seize the opportunity (in contrast to the post-political establishment that tries to quash any such moment). The fact that many populists, once in government, do not actually improve the lives of those they pretend to speak for is beside the point. Politics has been repressed, dissent against globalization and technocratic rule deemed illegitimate. Politics then returns in perverse forms.

Why? It is important to understand that the state, under the transformations wrought in the neoliberal period, is tasked merely with servicing the needs of the global market, and with managing a multicultural society at home, through emphasis on tolerance and separation. To argue that the rules of globalization should be broken – for instance, to protect workers – is seen as a childish or irresponsible desire for "simple" solutions, as against the complex technocracy of the post-political. Anger and hatred are *verboten*. Revindications that come from "below" or from "outside" are only permitted if they take the form of humanitarian pleading: *we are victims, please rescue us.* So, concerts to "save Africa" or campaigns to protect women from harassment or initiatives to help refugees are acknowledged (even if no substantial action is ever taken). Self-assertion, however, is a no-no. As the sociologist Wolfgang Streeck put it, "[n]othing polarizes the capitalist societies of today more than the debates about the *necessity and legitimacy* of national politics." In reference to the way the boundaries between class struggle and culture war have become blurred, Streeck additionally notes how "interests and identities fuse and give rise to mutual hostility of a pitch such as we have not seen since the end of the Cold War."[23] Consequently, those who wish for the state to take a role in social development, in guaranteeing more equitable outcomes, end up ranged against the guardians of the post-political order; this conflict is then misleadingly recast as "nativists vs cosmopolitans," in the interests of making the latter appear Zen and rational, while painting the former as irrational malcontents.

Of course, elites reflexively break all these rules when urgent measures are needed to stabilize the system. The trillion-dollar bailouts in 2008 already seemed extraordinary, and created fractures in the post-political edifice. A decade later, the measures which met the Covid-19 crisis, such as closing borders, housing the homeless or income guarantees, demolished it entirely. The transformation of French president Emmanuel Macron is illustrative of established elites breaking their own rules under the force of crisis: first, he was the energetic and modernizing force who was going to reform France and save the EU/liberalism/globalization; then, by the end of 2019, he was a cowed man, hobbled by over a year of intense social protest and strikes; by mid-2020 he was talking of the "end of this cycle of globalization" for its "undermining of democracy."[24]

At the End of the End of History, it's not so much that "politics is back." Instead, it is that various forms of anti-politics have been kicking down the door of post-politics. At present, though, it is elites who are moving on from neoliberal management to something else. The task of any wider politicization still falls to radical forces.

3.8 The contours of anti-politics

What then is this "anti-politics" that has been trying to kick down the door? Scattered descriptions in the literature describe it as a popular mood of discontent, mistrust and cynicism. Others conceive it as a strategy of depoliticization, or, on another plane, as a discursive system, best exemplified in Blairite "Third Way" politics. But these latter descriptions incorrectly approximate anti-politics to post-politics. One extensive study, already cited[25], defines anti-politics as negative sentiment toward the activities of formal politics (tolerating, canvassing, listening, negotiating, and compromising) as well as its key institutions and actors (politicians, parties, elections, parliaments, councils and governments). The authors are careful to state that anti-politics is something less than negativity toward democracy itself, but more than negativity toward particular actors or institutions. Simultaneously, it is more active than apathy, and instead rests on the ignition of people's passions.

This gets us halfway there. Anti-politics indeed must be seen as an *active* rejection of politics, and not a passive "dropping out." But these approaches all suffer from an over-identification with the spaces and arena of formal politics as such. Anti-politics is consequently seen as a negative force, something that makes government more difficult and leads to support for populists. Eliane Glaser's *Anti-Politics* is a case in point: it is visibly motivated by frustration with the way anti-politics or populism ends up victimizing the Left. While it undoubtedly does, the approach comes off as a self-interested complaint about the loss of authority of the institutional liberal left. A definition of anti-politics cannot start from the desire to defend the particular forms and processes of liberal democracy; this would end up classing all radical politics as anti-political as well. The irruption of social movements and protest, of revolutionary vanguards, would also fall into the bucket of the anti-political. Anti-politics instead requires a more adaptive definition, hinged on an energetic notion of politicization as the essence of democracy.

So, to state our position and definition: politics at its most essential is the demand for reordering statuses and upending hierarchies. It is a demand for equality; it is even the basic notion of contestation. The "end of politics" is a transhistorical tendency, for wherever politics emerges, there are forces trying to moderate it, ground it, smash it, transcend it or foreclose it. Politics is therefore of relative rarity. *Anti*-politics then emerges in earnest as a visible, regular concern at the End of the End of History. The strategy of depoliticization known as post-politics breeds an angry reaction: the institutions of formal politics come to be rejected by citizens. At the End of the End of History, anti-politics becomes the predominant force. The rejection of the old consensus politics (post-politics) and its precise forms, modes and representatives, does more than just express a negative mood. It also takes aim at political authority and representation itself; it is thus that *politics itself* is rejected, tout court.

Anti-politics can come from below or from above, as an organic development within the masses, or from above, from existing political representatives or new, counter-elites (as we will see in Chapter 5). Anti-politics, in its opposition to the managerial consensus, appears to politicize. When populists assert an antagonism between people and elites, and promise to "drain the swamp," that is an elementary politicization, for it stipulates division, instead of consensus, disruption instead of business-as-usual. However, anti-politics also takes aim at political authority itself, at the very possibility of representation. This inability to vest any power with legitimacy is truly anti-political, and is devastating not only for liberal democracy, but also for radical-democratic movements. Thus, while anti-politics is incipiently politicizing, it simultaneously carries the danger of the obviation of all politics, high and low. This clears the way for authoritarian rule.

Chapter 4

Neoliberal Order Breakdown Syndrome

The liberal wing of the establishment has had a tough time adjusting to the End of the End of History. A tougher time, indeed, than any other section of society. The two events that above all else caused much of the commentariat and the pundit class to lose their bearings entirely were the 2016 referendum in Britain, and Donald Trump's election as president in the US.

Trump's election was simply too much for much of the American liberal establishment to take. The MSNBC presenter Rachel Maddow provides perhaps the clearest example of someone who, with respect to Trump, "cannot even," to use the internet slang of the age. Dispensing with the need for evidence Maddow has consistently alleged that Trump is a Russian agent, under the control of Russian president Vladimir Putin, taking Russian press briefings and directing American missile attacks against targets chosen by the Russian president himself.[1]

Maddow is not alone. There is a deeper malaise in the American commentariat, affecting even the composed papers of record, *The Washington Post* and *The New York Times.* Differing stripes of the broad political center have pulled together in defense of the establishment, and against the apparent historical aberration presented by the erratic Republican president. Never mind all the massacres, support for dictators and corrupt practices carried out in and through American institutions over the decades. What the US was facing with Trump was truly intolerable, illiberal and undemocratic. These reactions earned the term "Trump Derangement Syndrome." But the phenomenon is wider and deeper than just that. In the UK, Remainers – a vocal minority who refused to accept the results of the 2016 referendum – panicked about the UK "leaving

Europe" (suggesting that, somehow, the country would no longer belong to the same continent). Not only that, but hysteria was whipped up over impending food shortages, over Cambridge Analytica warping minds, or any manner of imaginable disaster scenarios. In place of any good-faith attempt to understand the deeper changes in politics that precipitated the vote to leave the EU, "respectable" commentators, pundits and politicians engaged in a whole range of outré claims, from pointing the finger at Russia to blaming social media, lathered in insults to the ordinary voter. Truth, balance, proportionality – even adulthood – were jettisoned. What really explained the moment was...Harry Potter.[2] Even several years later, the liberal response to these events remains marked by a melancholic nostalgia for the recent past. For a social stratum that has cast itself as the moral and intellectual guardian of society and thus as a critic of power, it is remarkable to see the liberal establishment long for a vanished period prior to 2016 – a period that is not that distant from today. This nostalgia is paired with evasion of responsibility. The liberal establishment, in the ascendancy until very recently, proved unwilling to countenance the part played by the political class in creating today's conditions. Their monsters – Trump or Brexit – seemed to appear out of nowhere.

These hysterical reactions to the End of the End of History are merely the sharp end of what is better termed "Neoliberal Order Breakdown Syndrome" (NOBS): the inability of the liberal establishment to accept, explain or respond to political change.[3] This collection of symptoms is a key pathology of contemporary politics. Its characteristic tone of hysteria and catastrophism is driven by a horror at the dislocation of an old order and a terror at liberals' own impending loss of status. For commentators in particular, their privileged position as "politics knowers" has been challenged, to great consternation.

NOBS has exposed the fundamental weakness of the dominant contemporary ideology – postmodern liberalism – and its inability to explain the politics of the present, or to reconcile any of its own numerous contradictions.[4] What happens when liberal claims to rule by expertise are exposed as providing sub-optimal outcomes? How is the desire for social harmony served by growing inequality? Why does the emphasis on tolerance seem never to extend to working-class habits and behavior?

In terms of the regional and sociological distribution of NOBS, we should note firstly that NOBS was not, and is not, a universal phenomenon across the globe. The neoliberal order is breaking down nearly everywhere, but the psychological reactions cataloged here are only manifest in certain places. It has been most acutely experienced in the UK and the US, where the hegemony of contemporary liberalism is strongest, and where it has latterly come under the sharpest challenge. Germany, to take a notable point of contrast, has been more or less unshaken by a force such as Euroscepticism. This is consistent with the fact that it has been spared some of the more abrupt economic dislocations of the past decade, because of its hegemonic position in the Union. The establishment there is able comfortably to laugh at the UK for wanting to leave the EU, or, for that matter, at Americans for being gun-toting reactionaries.[5] In those countries where NOBS has manifested itself, it has struck the upper reaches of the media, business circles, the arts, trade union bureaucrats, academia, centrist or left-leaning think tanks, civil servants and politicians from the Center-Left to the Center-Right. They all reacted in spasm at the closing of the End of History. NOBS also goes beyond just the powerful and influential. Anyone with high cultural capital in the general orbit of center-left parties – namely, the Democratic Party in the US and the Labour Party, Greens, Liberal Democrats and Scottish National Party in the UK – has been more likely to exhibit NOBS. While this section of society may not see themselves as the *real* economic winners (i.e. the top 1 percent of the income distribution), they benefited from an order in which they retained at least cultural authority if not wealth.

There is a paradox here. This section of society assumes their views and predilections are common sense, while at the same time feeling constantly embattled. Another way to put this is that, while the "liberal package" (combining elements such as cosmopolitanism, respect for expertise, individualism, an emphasis on personal ethics) is culturally hegemonic, liberals refuse to acknowledge their own hegemony. The liberal always has her back to the wall. While their views find home in the newspapers of record, they feel submerged under a tsunami of tabloid content. They flaunt their commitment to tolerance and diversity, but balk at the expression of non-liberal views from fellow citizens. While they may often be critical of the government of the day – often critical of it "from the left" – they are fundamentally at ease and at home in the contemporary world; they have done well out of current arrangements. Moreover, their political identities are founded on the idea of being "the good guys." A less charitable interpretation would even argue that their interest in politics only exists insofar as it allows them to cast themselves as ethical actors. All this means hegemonic liberals could be moral critics from positions of relative comfort, content in the knowledge that the world would not really move against them, or even change appreciably.

But then it did. This did not come entirely out of the blue, though. Today's NOBS can be compared with its precursors in the 2000s and early 2010s. Indeed, in 2003 the neoconservative pundit Charles Krauthammer, defending the Republican president of the day from liberal attack, coined the term "Bush Derangement Syndrome" to refer to "the acute onset of paranoia in otherwise normal people in reaction to the policies, the presidency – nay – the very existence of [President] George W. Bush."[6] Bush was, of course, later redeemed in the eyes of a surprising number of liberals. This was due to a combination of nostalgia for Bush's brand of Republicanism , his friendship with the righteous Obamas, and an appreciation for his newfound artistic sensibilities.[7]

In Italy, throughout the 2000s, the moderate Left was horrified at Silvio Berlusconi and often painted themselves as partisans fighting Berlusconi's "fascism." What makes NOBS different, however, is that it afflicts a much wider section of society. It is found as much on the Center-Right as on the Center-Left; and it reaches deeper too, as the professional middle class has expanded and become more politicized (see Chapter 7).

NOBS, then, is the paradigmatic response on the part of the liberal establishment to the End of the End of History. It is quite possible that readers, particularly those in the US or the UK, will have seen NOBS symptoms up close, as friends, family members or acquaintances have delivered their "hot takes" on recent history. These ideas are unlikely to be infectious (at least not without sustained contact with *The Guardian* or *The New York Times*), but one does risk acquiring secondary-contact symptoms of annoyance, frustration and severe deflation by entering into conversation with them.

To help those whose loved ones may have contracted NOBS, in this chapter we try to give a more systematic anatomy of the nine symptoms[8], grouped into three sets – the inability to *accept*, to *explain* and to *respond* to political change. In the final section of the chapter we offer an explanation as to why NOBS may have come to represent a central part of the "common sense" of the liberal establishment.[9]

4.1 The inability to accept political change

The first symptom of NOBS is often a basic incredulity: the mechanism of denial. Unlike the stages of grief, however, denial is not followed by bargaining or acceptance (even if members of the liberal establishment may feel anger and/or depression for reasons related to their loss of political influence and status). Brexit provides perhaps the signal example. There has been a

Table 4.1: The symptoms of Neoliberal Order Breakdown Syndrome (NOBS)

Diagnostic area	Characteristic symptoms
Inability to *accept* political change	• Incredulity at, or denial of, political change • Refusal to accept responsibility for creating contemporary conditions
Inability to *explain* political change	• Model of political causation replaced by cognitive or informational theories; e.g. social media, or Russia-based conspiracy theories. Unwillingness to attribute agency to citizens/voters
Inability to *respond to* political change	• Catastrophism and hysteria • Nostalgia for very recent past • Elite persecution complex, hypersensitivity to criticism • Infantilism, expressed as childishness, tweeness or desire for authority to quickly resolve problems • Hectoring, moralization • Repetition compulsion

repeated insistence that the 2016 referendum result can simply be denied through, e.g., arguing that 52 percent is an insufficient majority or that the referendum was never meant to be binding.

Perhaps the vanguard of this tendency has been the British podcast-cum-movement the Remainiacs, who appropriated the iconography of The Ramones and adopted the rallying cry of "Ho hey, let's stay." A range of members of parliament, top lawyers, journalists, sitcom stars, writers and indie musicians have joined them in arguing that something fundamentally irrational happened in 2016, and asserting that the correct response ought to be to move from astonished amusement to righteous anger, in order to subvert the referendum result.

Similarly, Jeremy Corbyn's ascension to the leadership of the Labour Party and the subsequent influx of new left-wing members was treated as incomprehensible by much of the commentariat. Janan Ganesh of the *Financial Times* opted for a simple, clear explanation of the rise of Corbyn, tweeting in August 2016: "You can do analysis of Corbyn and his 'movement' (I have done it) but the essence of the whole thing is that they are just thick as pigshit."[10] Somewhat more developed analyses have dismissed Corbynism as a cult, likening Corbyn (and Trump) to the Manson Family (*Guardian* columnist Hadley Freeman); describing Corbyn's Labour Party as a "glorified protest group with cult trimmings" (Tony Blair); or straightforwardly labeling Corbynism a "cult venerating the messiah" (former Labour MP Bridget Prentice).[11] At core, there is a refusal to admit that political developments may be related to the loss of legitimacy of a set of ideals (neoliberal economics, meritocracy, individualism, etc.) that these commentators would endorse. The idea that an alternative vision might prove popular, capable of rousing passions, was not computable. After all, post-politics was meant to have extinguished all enthusiasms. Affective ties in politics could only be atavistic or irrational, and thus anyone promising sweeping change must, by definition, be fundamentally problematic. Moreover these liberals had been content to play their roles as moral critics "from the left". To find that they had been outflanked on that side meant their sense of political coordinates became disoriented. They were now, suddenly, "centrists," or better yet, merely just "sensible."

Unlike followers of populism, with their worship of political leaders, liberal pundits see themselves as above the influence of cheap charisma. Yet we already saw in the last chapter how Bill Clinton's saxophone-playing was eulogized, how he became, as Toni Morrison put it, "our first black president" (despite, of course, his policies resulting in the mass incarceration of the US' black citizens).[12] Tony Blair attempted to match his US counterpart by embracing "Cool Britannia" and inviting Oasis' Noel Gallagher to Downing Street, while Barack Obama's family photos warmed the hearts of liberals. More recently, personalized politics has made a heartthrob of French strongman Emmanuel Macron and even led some to identify a "Justin Trudeau effect," such is the charm and handsomeness of the Canadian prime minister.[13] Building up leaders on the basis of personal attributes is not solely the preserve of populists.

This hypocrisy is part of a wider attempt by cultural and political elites to write themselves out of the story. The liberal establishment evinces an unwillingness to take responsibility for creating the conditions that lead people to yearn for a world in which their voices might be heard. If Trump and Brexit were supposedly the revolt of the "left behind," who left them behind? Who was in charge while former industrial areas were allowed to fall into decrepitude, as the metropolis boomed and the hinterlands rotted? Even a high priest of neoliberalism, economist and former US Treasury secretary Larry Summers, has taken to warning about the fragility and dependency induced by global supply chains, as if it had not been he who orchestrated offshoring to China. Typical of this evasive attitude, he now piously intones that globalization was too much "for the benefit of those in Davos, and too little for the benefit of those in Detroit or Dusseldorf."[14]

4.2 The inability to explain political change

In conjunction with a refusal to *accept* change, NOBS almost always manifests as an inability to *explain* political change. This is hardly surprising since the liberal establishment tends to operate with a model of politics in which naked defense of social interests is taboo. Policies are couched in the language of consensus, scientific evidence and ethics. To the extent that politics features conflict, it is as pantomime, or worse, a tedious morality play: us, noble saviors; you, *Voldemorts*.

One illustration of this process by which politics is psychologically characterized as a morality struggle between good and evil is the surprising persistence of *The West Wing* – an idealized model of "doing politics." Many liberals turned to binge-watching the show (which finished airing in 2006) on streaming websites as a safety blanket in the Trump years, seeing Martin Sheen's Nobel Prize-winning economist President Jed Bartlett as the leader they want but cannot have. *The West Wing* represented an ideal of a more principled, more intelligent politics. As *The Washington Post* put it: "Revisiting the series on Netflix means revisiting moderation, collegiality, principles over partisanship."[15] Comfort TV as therapy for a Trump presidency speaks to this yearning for morally upstanding leaders, for the most principled of people to make the best of decisions for the best of reasons.[16] Moral explanations grounded in "common decency" come to stand in for an analysis of power relations.

This is of a part with the way the liberal establishment evinces little, if any, belief in political causation. Instead, *things just happen*, with one political event following another in a random walk. For the NOBS-afflicted liberal, recent political history is *just one fucking thing after another*, a catastrophe that sees wreckage piled upon wreckage. In this process, responsibility is passed onto external actors with the result that increasingly conspiratorial explanations come to the fore. Allegations of foreign interference – normally ridiculed as paranoia, when voiced by say, Serbians or Venezuelans about their own political systems – have become an accepted explanation for political events in the United States, the most powerful country on Earth.

This is clearest in the astonishing longevity of accounts of Russian meddling in the 2016 presidential election. This widely accepted explanation for the election of Trump only began to dissipate in early 2019 when hitherto heroic anti-Trump warrior Robert Mueller reported that there had been no interference. The Covid-19 crisis seemed to have done away with "Russiagate," only for the protests in response to the police murder of George Floyd in 2020 to offer yet another opportunity to revive Cold War tropes. One of Obama's former National Security Advisors, Susan Rice, argued that she "would not be surprised to learn that [Russians] have fomented some of these extremists on both sides using social media."[17]

It is commonplace in US politics to present the Kremlin as the point of coordination of an extraordinarily sophisticated campaign of bots and social media sabotage, and to talk of Trump's "subservience" to Putin.[18] At the same time, one of the veritable strengths of this analysis is that any event or action of Trump's – as well as the process of his impeachment – is just yet more evidence of Russian power.[19] It is an unfalsifiable theory.

Another explanatory failure can be seen in the campaign of Hillary Rodham Clinton. The obsessive polling and statistical modeling of Clinton's campaign manager Robby Mook infamously resulted in a strategy at odds with the advice of activists on the ground, including that Clinton finish her campaign in Arizona rather than Wisconsin. Mook concluded that it was a "waste of time and energy" to try to persuade undecided voters or to go to rural areas.[20] The superior wisdom of the algorithm stands in for any political understanding. Agency and political causation are discarded in favor of conspiracy theorizing or, alternatively, a series of correlations and regression models.

The only real explanatory factor in a NOBS-afflicted vision of contemporary politics is the media. Given that liberals tend to trust the media more than the general public,[21] they are predictably prone to overstate its influence. Thus we find the liberal establishment fetishizing *dis*information, such as when it blames social media manipulation for political events. The syndrome has ravaged the brains of the commentariat to such an extent that they have largely been willing to junk even central Enlightenment ideals such as truth and facts. Reflecting a wider cultural tendency in the immediate aftermath of Brexit and Trump, the Oxford English Dictionary declared "post-truth" its 2016 international word of the year, while the Society for the German Language followed suit, selecting *postfaktisch* ("post-factual").[22] This emerged in tandem with a burgeoning pop-politics literature on "post-truth," as well as academic investigations into the topic.[23] Something of a moral panic took hold of the entire pundit class with the Cambridge Analytica scandal, in which the company had used mined Facebook data to create psychographic profiles of users at whom to target political advertising. There have been a range of suggested responses to this panic, including Macron's plan for a European agency to combat fake news at a continental level – although of course the issue is of personal concern to Macron himself following the "Macron leaks" scandal in which his emails were hacked in the final hours of the French presidential election campaign.[24]

It should go without saying that at root is a view of media consumers as gullible, easily conned and essentially without agency. Those pushing these cognitive theories probably never asked themselves whether they had been swayed by political advertisements as they idly scrolled on Facebook; the answer would surely be no. But they would not extend the same faith to most citizens. The idea that citizens could be trusted to vote "correctly" also comes under strain. These elitist attitudes have allowed epistocrats and gnosocrats – those who believe that society should be ruled by its most knowledgeable and intelligent citizens (i.e. themselves) – to come out of the shadows and solemnly conclude that tests of political knowledge must sadly be introduced so as to save democracy from itself, oblivious to how far their own arguments echo the venerable line of establishment anti-suffrage arguments.[25]

4.3 The inability to respond to political change

If political change is neither accepted nor explained, it is almost impossible to formulate a coherent response to it. The liberal establishment has preferred to portray contemporary politics as a "nasty game" in which they are the abused and wronged victims. Here we encounter another characteristic symptom of NOBS: a persecution complex among some of the more influential and well-off members of society.

In the US context we can see, for instance, the notion of the "Bernie Bro" as a dangerous threat to supporters of Hillary Clinton in 2016 – or Elizabeth Warren in 2020. We see the self-idealization of anti-Trump liberalism as the #Resistance, invoking the authority of anti-fascist guerrilla struggle. In Britain, MPs developed their own complex: protesters who called ex-Tory MP Anna Soubry a Nazi, a traitor, and a fascist outside parliament had to plead guilty to causing the one-time leader of the "The Independent Group for Change" "harassment, alarm, or distress."[26] In this way, speech acts are hysterically re-coded as threats at the same level as physical violence and intimidation. The consequence of this presentation of elite-as-victim is to allow relatively privileged members of society to mask their real economic and political power, and instead portray themselves as worthy of popular sympathy. This "elite persecution complex," then, manifests itself as hypersensitivity to criticism of any sort. Politics has traditionally been rough-and-tumble; only the post-politics of the End of History allowed the intelligentsia to think it wasn't, or shouldn't be, this way.

Psychological escape from this new state of affairs is had through nostalgia for the very recent past. Well-heeled liberals do not see themselves as winners but rather as critics, bravely speaking truth to power. They thus allow themselves to be nostalgic for a time of smoother, calmer government. In the UK, the 2012 Olympics are often described in misty-eyed terms as "a high point for a self-confident and outward-looking United

Kingdom."[27] The American liberal's desire for a return of the Obama years is a recurring issue. One high-profile journalist opined that Obama should be brought in to calm rioters in May 2020 after the death of George Floyd – oblivious to the fact that Black Lives Matters originated in similar circumstances during Obama's presidency.[28]

Despite its proximity in time, this dreamed-of recent past is impossible to recapture. Instead, mired in deep pessimism, liberals resort to pompous declarations of the terribleness of the present. Scaling the heights of preposterous catastrophism, former chess grandmaster and outspoken liberal Garry Kasparov asserted in July 2018, "I'm ready to call this the darkest hour in the history of the American presidency. Let me know if you can think of any competition."[29] Nostalgia toward the past and dark fantasy about the future led Remainers in the UK to espouse the idea Brexit would threaten school dinners, cause deaths due to insulin shortages, lead the economy to contract by 8 percent in a single year, and create shortages of bacon and mozzarella.[30] Who knew it was possible to be at once portentous and trite?

Allied to nostalgia and catastrophism is a repetition compulsion, whereby liberals replay (often in comically similar terms) key political processes, hoping for a different outcome. This mechanism has clearly been at work in calls for a second referendum in the UK, and can be observed in the Italian *Partito Democratico* aping the US Democrats' visibly failed strategy: doubling down on establishment liberalism while their working-class base withers. The fate of other formerly social-democratic parties across Europe tells the tale too. In fact, any number of the examples cited throughout this chapter are subject to pathological repetition, irrespective of consequence – part of a political obsessive-compulsive disorder.

Standing in for any "political" response to political change, the last few years have instead witnessed a striking infantilism on the part of the liberal establishment. This has included childishness (the constant Harry Potter references[31] or the Donald Trump baby balloon used on protests in London) and infantilism (e.g., profane slogans such as "Bollocks to Brexit" or "Fuck Boris"). In a more figurative – and more dangerous – sense, infantilism expresses itself in a desire for an external authority to resolve political problems. NOBS-sufferers turn to unelected figures, such as former FBI director James Comey or UK Supreme Court judge Lady Hale, both celebrated for their bravery in standing up to the political foes of establishment liberalism. A similar response is seen in the desire for Facebook to solve the fake news moral panic through tighter controls. The traditional gatekeepers can feel the world slipping through their fingers and so appeal to any authority, including the oligarchic social media giant, to stem the flow. The childishness and tweeness come off as a refusal to take politics seriously, and stand in painful contradiction to the hysterical warnings of impending doom. Pussy hats against fascism? Really?

Defensiveness, rooted in a sense of one's own waning influence, often leads to a moralizing response: not just hectoring and finger-wagging, but condescension too. In her only truly poetic formulation, Hillary Clinton's famous "basket of deplorables," as she called (half of) Trump's supporters, captured this beautifully. In the US, so as the rest of the world; we see the same deplorables in different baskets. The left-liberal journalist Laurie Penny, in the aftermath of the 2016 referendum, blamed Leave voters' "frightened, parochial lizard-brain," while Paul Mason declared the 2019 election result to be "a victory of the old over the young, racists over people of color, selfishness over the planet."[32] Across the traditional political class there has been the cultivation of this progressive contempt. It's old-fashioned elitism, justified on "woke" grounds. Since the people are basically just idiot rubes, their opinions can be dismissed. As Clinton put it, they're "racist, sexist, homophobic, xenophobic – Islamophobic – you name it."[33] When those attitudes hold, instead of seeking to persuade people otherwise – or asking why these prejudices exist – complacent dismissal is the chosen course of (in)action. The liberal has a clean conscience for *their* hatred, and is free to punish – economically, politically or culturally – the people for their backwardness. The idea (encountered in the previous chapter) that repression of hatred, of political passions, might have a role in eruptions of bigotry, is never countenanced.

In sum, then, we can outline the core symptoms of NOBS: a fevered inability on the part of the liberal establishment to *accept* political change, leading to incredulity, denial and a refusal to take responsibility; an inability to *explain* political change, replacing any credible understanding of political causation with a facile fetishization of disinformation or lack of knowledge on the part of voters; an inability to *respond* to political change, with reactions marked variously by an elite persecution complex, nostalgia for a very recent past, catastrophism, repetition compulsion, infantilization and moralization.

4.4 Explaining NOBS

To explain NOBS we have to venture further into the mindset of the liberal in the halcyon years prior to 2016. As we saw in the introduction, this mental world offered little stimulation. The End of History was marked by a "retromania," in which music, art, television and film were mired in nostalgia, recycling and repetition, and inflected with a low-key and cynical pessimism. One writer astutely characterized the landscape as "endlessness and onwardness" to refer, for example, to the way long-running TV series or film franchises see the appearance of the same characters and fictional universes, over and over.[34] In short, nothing was new: we had run out of ideas. And so we looked backward for forms of divertissement, or to the impending end of the world, for motivating cultural ideas.

While the boring, repetitive nature of culture during the End of History has been sharply diagnosed, those treatments do less to explain what motivated this cultural exhaustion, and to tie it to the world of politics. Looking back on the first decades of the twenty-first century, it is now clear that the culture of Western Europe and in particular North America was defined (and distorted) by the absence of any horizon of History, by the potential of a fundamental change in social organization. Hopes for socialism, communism staked out a different future; utopias existed, even if only – at the very least – in our minds. The absence of another, higher plane of history in front of us meant we were stuck in an eternal present.

Perhaps we don't even have to go that far. Simply the absence of different *capitalist* regimes, beyond the reigning neoliberalism, was enough to dull imaginations within the Western bubble. The foreclosure of contestation produced a deadening stability. If you tacked to the left, you could maybe see things getting slightly, slowly worse as we slouched to eco-apocalypse. If you were on the pro-business right, slightly, slowly better in statistics on global trade and declining infant mortality. Either way, there was no drama. The things we had then were here to stay, forever.

Even the categories used to understand politics had become zombified. Instead of starting with society as it is, with people's actual frustrations and hopes and interests, liberals looked at things from the top-down, using the same marketing categories created for vote-getting machine politics. So it was assumed, for example, that, if someone was a Labour voter, they were an urban liberal or an industrial worker or ethnic minority; or they were a non-voter, and therefore didn't matter much at all. There are pre-set boxes, and the population fit into them. Through opinion polling and focus groups, the "customer's" needs were understood, and so the political party-as-brand could orient its messaging to the target audience appropriately. The composite image of past behavior and current preferences predicted future behavior. Politics, then, was a process of managing any unrealistic expectations voters might have, while singing the praises of manifestly mediocre technocrats as pragmatists who knew what was possible and what was not.

As political parties became increasingly dependent on the state rather than civil society, the distance between parties and voters increased while those between parties themselves decreased. In the words of Peter Mair, "parties become the government's representative in society, rather than society's bridgehead in the state."[35] Political commentators grew accustomed to a peculiar sort of politics: near consensus among the political class, a distant and disinterested citizenry, and an increasing focus on geographically concentrated centers of government ("Westminster," "Washington," "Brussels"). Heated discussion of "polarization" in US politics was mere window-dressing for narrow partisan politicking, or else represented cultural, not political, divisions. Of course, it was not just political commentators, but a whole raft of professionals working in NGOs, elite cultural institutions, the academy and so on who came to view society in this top-down manner: society as a passive, manipulable object.

At the same time, a particular vision of "the right way of doing politics," which fit comfortably with the interests and proclivities of the liberal pundit, filled this yawning void between the electorate and formal politics. It was essentially the mindset of the professionalized Oxbridge PPE grad, Énarque or Beltway type who, as lanyard-wearing special advisors or interchangeable PR advisers and suits-as-politicians, dominated the politics of the era. In this context the political party was reduced to a location for the careers of ambitious young graduates too lazy or dim to become investment bankers. In lockstep with the celebration of competence came the expectation of an affect of a middle class etiquette, incorporating solemn professionalism and decorum. Anger, for instance, was excluded from the set of legitimate political affects, which is why what the writer Amber A'Lee Frost called the "Dirtbag Left" attracted such opprobrium: it looked to reject civility and sobriety in tone, and instead embrace vulgarity.[36]

We discussed in previous chapters the elite concern about popular apathy. Critiques of mass disengagement usually had a moral tone, suggesting that anyone who was not fired-up enough by Blairite or Clintonite platitudes to go and vote was not only missing the chance to have their say but was also letting everyone else down by being a bad citizen.[37] The breakdown of the neoliberal order and the strange politics it has thrown up means that many would no doubt prefer to see citizens go back to being merely "bad," rather than angry, irrational and undisciplined, as they are now seen.

Floating in the placid waters of a politics without the people and a culture without history, liberal establishments have now been thoroughly jarred by the return of politics. The fact politics reappears as *anti*-politics is particularly threatening, because it throws into question the status and professional interests of that section of society that has the greatest affective investment in discredited liberal institutions. The masses have disinvested themselves; business elites are ultimately interested in the bottom line, leaving political elites and middle-class professionals trying desperately to hold on to a post-political world that is slipping away.

Chapter 5

Politics Against Itself: Varieties of Anti-Politics

Though "anti-politics" seemed to be winning, the first stages of the Covid-19 crisis provided a brief interruption to Neoliberal Order Breakdown Syndrome. The authority of scientific expertise was bolstered by the pandemic. But this proved short-lived, technocracy's return showing itself to be more of an end-of-life rally.[1] Anti-political movements continued to challenge political establishments and the "rally round the flag" effect established during the height of the crisis was shortly followed by mass protest. The nature of anti-politics, though, is that it tends to compound the undermining of political authority, because those politicians and movements that wield it often refuse to seize authority themselves.

The move from the End of History to the End of the End of History is in one sense the story of anti-politics gaining the upper hand over post-politics. As seen in Chapter 3, traditional elites are in a panic over populism. This is best understood as anti-politics "from above." It is our contention here that anti-politics mostly comes "from below," from the citizenry. It can take various forms, from right to left to politically amorphous. When these anti-political energies are captured by political entrepreneurs, especially those with existing links to formal politics, that is anti-politics from above: populism. In what follows, we will catalog the various forms of anti-politics, focusing mainly on anti-politics from below.

To declare that "they are all corrupt" is possibly the most essential instance of anti-politics today. Its nature as a politically ambivalent complaint is of a piece with the post-ideological times of the post-Cold War world. Moreover, its capacity to denude democracy of any authority – because political autonomy means the freedom to be corrupt, too – means it is also the most dangerous. We argue that anti-corruption politics has two possible end results: either post-politics or authoritarianism. Given the centrality of claims of corruption to anti-politics, and the importance of its consequences, we start the chapter by examining anti-corruption and give it the most space. The next three forms we deal with are emergences on the political Left, which we call "horizontalism," "revolutionism" and "left defeatism." Finally, we turn to anti-politics from above and examine how counter-elites were formed in different countries around the world, appropriating anti-political energies to advance national-populist projects.

5.1 Anti-corruption

Foreign Policy dubbed 2019 "A Year of Global Protest," citing the wave of "leaderless" movements in Ecuador, Bolivia, Chile, Haiti, France, Iraq, Iran, Sudan, Hong Kong, Indonesia and beyond. Although each demonstration was sparked by different social phenomena, the magazine identified universal targets: "corruption, political dysfunction, and a general discontent with economic stewardship that seems to offer little promise for a lost generation."[2] Separately, the BBC sought to identify what, if anything, 2019's protests all had in common. Corruption was cited alongside inequality, the climate and freedom.[3]

Well before 2019, Italy was pioneering new forms of anti-corruption protest; after all, the country expresses contemporary, degenerative political tendencies earlier and better than elsewhere. The Italian First Republic was brought down by the investigation of corruption and ensuing scandal in the early 1990s, paving the way for Silvio Berlusconi (see Chapter 6 for a full account). One inheritor of that anti-political, anti-corruption moment was a curious phenomenon called the Five Star Movement (M5S), founded by a comedian, Beppe Grillo.

Two years prior to the party's formation, Grillo created what he called "V Day," held on September 8, 2007. Five million were said to have participated in the event organized around three political demands: an electoral system allowing voters directly to choose representatives rather than voting for party lists; two-term limits; and a "cleaning of parliament" whereby candidates convicted of crimes would be barred from office. More than 300,000 signatures were collected. V Day – V for *vaffanculo*, or "go fuck yourself" – was conceived as standing against Berlusconi and *Berlusconismo*. And yet, the organizers ended up facing allegations of demagoguery, populism and anti-politics – precisely some of the charges regularly thrown at Berlusconi himself. Grillo answered these claims arguing that he was merely against the political class, not politics as such. Nevertheless, Grillo refused to identify himself with either Left or Right, and instead put himself forward as an intermediator, representing the whole people against the corrupt elite.

In what can be viewed as an ironic – or depressingly predictable – turn of events, M5S found itself in government a decade later with the Lega, a party that had pioneered anti-corruption populism in the early 1990s, albeit having a very different background to M5S.[4] In 2019, a year after the election that birthed the anti-political Lega-M5S government coalition, the Lega leader, Matteo Salvini, proposed new elections as Lega had risen in the polls at the expense of M5S (possibly as the latter no longer functioned as a catch-all vehicle for protest). Grillo opposed new elections, arguing M5S must instead "resist the barbarians" (i.e. the anti-immigration Lega), by allying with the M5S's erstwhile enemy, the establishment center-left Democrats. Five Star's railing against corruption and the political class ended up with Grillo's baby very much part of it. "Anti-corruption" demonstrated itself to provide no firm foundation for building power.

But anti-corruption politics was not always such a post-ideological catch-all for popular discontent. Throughout the Cold War, the politicization of corruption was seen as a weapon of socialist or national liberation movements against elites; consequently, Western powers largely ignored it, worrying it was a dangerous implement to handle. In the Eastern bloc, meanwhile, anti-corruption discourse was highly prevalent, but exactly because it was safe. It was viewed as a depoliticized manner of criticizing the government. One might note that anti-corruption's currency in contemporary China might be explained the same way.

It was only at the end of the Cold War that anti-corruption emerged from its pre-history. Western capitalist interests weaponized the discourse as a means of breaking up the Soviet system. Corruption was held by the "New World Order" to be a form of protectionism: an arrangement by which close personal relations between state agents and corporations are required to conduct business is prohibitive to outsiders. To further Western economic interests, the ties maintained by the post-Soviet *nomenklatura* had to be broken. Anti-corruption discourse at the End of History thus became a tool of neoliberalism. "Transparency" is the watchword, code for pro-market arrangements under which public power is prevented from extracting rents from corporations. It is a means of restricting the interventionist or developmentalist state. Although it seems a self-evident good, "transparency" guarantees not political autonomy, but the autonomy of capital.

But how does this relate to our concern here – anti-corruption as a form of anti-politics from below? Well, by a cunning of history, popular anti-corruption protests have a tendency to result in just the sort of post-political and technocratic management favored by institutions such as the IMF and World Bank. That isn't always the outcome, of course. In other cases, anti-corruption's delegitimation of the political class ends up exploding democratic political authority as such. Authoritarian populists then sweep to power. Here we will look at several cases, most of which lead to one of these two outcomes.

Eastern Europe is the primary site for these dynamics today. This should be of no surprise, given anti-corruption's pre-history in the Eastern bloc, followed by the Western-led weaponization of anti-corruption in the early 1990s. The hated "privileges" the *nomenklatura* awarded themselves under really existing socialism became "corruption" in the post-communist world. And the culprits were often the same *nomenklatura* who had adapted to the new world by leveraging their relationship to the state for their own gain.

Corruption can be seen nakedly here as a consequence of the privatization of state assets. Perhaps, more abstractly, it can also be understood as a privatization of politics: citizens disengage from public institutions and wealthy elites turn public administration into their personal playthings. One early 1990s Polish minister for privatization even described the process as "when someone who does not know who the real owner is and does not know what it is really worth sells something to someone who does not have any money."[5] As a response to these historical developments, citizens in these countries believe there to be far more corruption now than prior to 1991. According to Transparency International's Corruption Perception Index, all countries but one in the Eastern Europe/Central Asia region score 45 or below (where 100 is cleanest), with prospects worsening in most of them in recent years. It is in just these societies that anti-corruption protests have exploded with the greatest frequency.

In Moldova, a $1.5bn bank fraud in 2015 led to the largest demonstrations since Moldova's independence from the Soviet Union in 1991. While there were divergent tendencies, including a left-wing presence and one plank favoring unification with Romania, many waved EU flags. The Dignity and Truth Platform Party that emerged from the demonstrations, and whose nucleus mobilized the demonstrations at the start, maintains a center-right pro-EU stance. The thrust of anti-corruption here is to become a "normal country" within the EU. The anti-politics of opposition to corruption lends itself to post-politics. Rather than overthrow institutions, the solution is that they should be transformed through the external pressures of EU membership.

In 2017, mass protests gripped Romania, with up to half a million on the streets countrywide, in the largest protests since Ceausescu's fall. The center-left government attempted to weaken anti-corruption laws in order to, it argued, "reduce overcrowding in prisons." Protests initially advanced a discourse of a "new" Romania, emphasizing youth, meritocracy, professionalism, respect for rules, multiculturalism and so on, against old clientelistic and corrupt practices. Protests targeted the governing PSD, slated as "the Red Plague," for being the embodiment of the political class.[6] But the protesters also sneered at PSD voters for being bought off by the party's social agenda of pensions and social security. At the same time, a more identifiably "populist" tendency emerged, declaring all parties to be the same.[7] These catch-all protests thus capture both of anti-corruption's inherent tendencies: one which leans toward a "modernizing" post-political agenda, and another with more explicitly anti-political notes.[8]

Perhaps the most striking case was in Hungary. In the infamous "Őszöd speech" by then-prime minister Ferenc Gyurcsány in 2006, the Socialist Party leader admitted to systematic lying and to having achieved nothing of note in 4 years in office. The ensuing mass protests, the first of their type since 1989, led to the delegitimation of the post-Soviet left-liberal governments. Viktor Orban's Fidesz party then gained a supermajority in 2010. Here, anti-politics established the basis for Orban to become the leading figure of "illiberal democracy" in Europe, providing a template for other authoritarian populists.

Most recently, in early 2020 Slovakia voted in a maverick anti-corruption campaigner who had made his name through various public stunts aimed at demonstrating political impunity. His (anti-)political party could not have a more blatant name: the Ordinary People party.[9]

Of course, anti-corruption politics are not restricted to Eastern Europe, nor are all cases necessarily anti-political. For instance, in the run-up to Lopez Obrador's victory in Mexico's election, AMLO – as he is known – railed against a corrupt and rapacious minority of business executives. But the context of the Mexican state's fragile legitimacy and its implication with the drug cartels, and AMLO's own leftist program, meant his opposition to the "mafia of power" took a more determinate political form, seeming to evade both post-political and anti-political tendencies.

Nigeria's politics have also been dominated by anti-corruption, with the 2019 election framed in terms of an ethno-cultural right against a technocratic center, represented by Muhammadu Buhari and Atiku Abubakar, respectively. Both, however, centered on anti-corruption, to the extent that the main two political forces could be said to represent a single ideological position.[10] Anti-corruption here serves evident post-political purposes, obviating ideological contestation, as well as more obviously cynical ends, such as when President Buhari (re-elected in 2019) cracked down on civil society, using anti-corruption rhetoric. Protests from below urging action against corruption were unable to break beyond this circumscribed politics, and an opportunity for politicization goes wanting.

While the term "state capture" was first used in reference to post-Soviet Central Asian republics, designating systemic political corruption in which private interests are able to direct state decision-making to a significant degree, it is in South Africa where it found its most brazen recent instantiation. The Guptas, a wealthy Indian family, developed an extremely intimate relationship with President Jacob Zuma. The civil society "Save South Africa" campaign protested state capture, urging accountability and transparency. The drive to rid the country of Zuma and his corrupt rule, though, never mobilized an alternative vision. It remained hamstrung by the weakness of the opposition, the demobilization and bureaucratization of trade unions and the African National Congress's stagnation and corruption. The opposition instead reduced politics to the sole aim of getting rid of Zuma through highlighting his corruption. The post-Zuma era thus represents no significant change from the status quo ante, and South African society continues its drift.[11] Constant scandal-mongering can be demoralizing. Indeed, that is one of the primary consequences of corruption itself, and, perhaps, one of its objectives. Italian Marxist Antonio Gramsci saw corruption as a means of exercising class power: "Between consent and force stands corruption/fraud (which is characteristic of certain situations when it is hard to exercise the hegemonic function, and when the use of force is too risky). This consists in procuring the demoralization and paralysis of the antagonist (or antagonists) by buying its leaders – either covertly, or, in cases of imminent danger, openly – in order to sow disarray and confusion in his ranks."[12] In buying people off to achieve your ends, the public realm becomes privatized. The effect is to quash hopes that public life might improve; citizens then withdraw from political participation.

In this way, corruption and anti-corruption jointly impede politicization. The former acts by divesting the populace from expectations that progressive change is achievable; the latter casts politics as inherently corrupt, and thus intractable. Anti-corruption politics then tend to suggest technocratic solutions ("transparency"), which only increase the distance between people and politics. When anti-corruption takes on a more populist guise instead, it tends toward authoritarianism. As with Italy, where liberals and the Left became obsessed with removing Berlusconi, the focus on Zuma in South Africa did not build power but only furthered depoliticization.

Perhaps, though, it should not be surprising that the theme of corruption recurs with such constancy today, when the ideological frameworks of the past – in South Africa's case, that of socialism and national liberation – are such empty shells. Protests against corruption tend not only to seize on the misappropriation of public funds, but – directly or indirectly – on the notion that politicians are not acting in the public interest, be it because they have been co-opted by *private* interests, or because they have opted to sell out. As such, the charge of corruption regularly acts as a metaphor for the denunciation of the gulf between politicians and citizens, and communicates the idea that the former are a class apart. The post-political era thus opens the door to the discourse on corruption.

At this point, it is worth examining what "corruption" really means in the modern world. The concept is premised on the separation of public and private interests. Private interests in market society are not commonly held to be pathological; indeed, the capitalist system is based on the free pursuit of them. However, the intrusion of private interests into the public realm of state and government is theoretically forbidden – it's called corruption. Yet in market society, it is impossible to create and protect a truly disinterested public realm, driven purely by republican virtue. Indeed, much corruption is tolerated and even legalized – see lobbying, for instance. Additionally, it is impossible to know how much corruption there is; by its nature it is occult. So while people are rightly shocked at corruption scandals, there is rarely a way of correlating popular anger with the existence of actual corruption. The former is relatively autonomous from the latter, which is to say, anti-corruption protest is not driven by the existence of corruption per se (much as shocking revelations often provide the spark).

Contrarily, outrage about corruption in politics can even be indicative of a healthy democratic attitude. If citizens operate on the assumption that politicians should generally act in the public interest – whatever other compromises happen along the way – the revelation that they *have not* indicates a public expectation that they *should have*. But what happens when that expectation becomes frayed to the limit? Or when the revelation of corruption does not merely break bonds of trust (between citizen and leader, and between leader and the republic), but acts as confirmation of cynicism? When anti-corruption politics operate on this basis, it declares that there can be no good government. Here the very possibility of faithful political representation is put into question, and legitimate political authority loses all foundation.

The exemplary case of these dynamics is found in Brazil's epochal political crisis starting with 2013's "June Days," some of the largest street demonstrations in the country's history. The crisis as of yet has no end date – a new one merely follows another.[13] We can, however, be extremely clear about the denouement: anti-corruption leads to right-wing, authoritarian populism.

In early June 2013, a series of demonstrations were held to protest a hike in metro and bus fares in São Paulo, South America's largest city. Organized by an autonomist, pro-free transport group (*Movimento Passe Livre*), the protests started off small. But as with so many similar events around the globe, wider revulsion at heavy police repression led to the demonstration broadening out – both in terms of absolute numbers and in the sectors and classes of society involved. Within a few weeks, over 2 million were on the streets across Brazil.

Demands broadened to include the funding of health and education, anti-corruption measures, gay rights and political reform. In sum, it spoke to a crisis of representation, as the growth in expectations that accompanied Brazil's boom in the preceding decade could no longer be satisfied. However, these were masses composed of various crowds, a few of which could be identified with a specific political tendency, but most not. The Left was fragmented between a Workers Party (PT) that had been in government for over a decade and emerged skeptical of the protests, and various non-PT parties, unions and movements. A strongly anti-political thrust began to gain traction within the demonstrations, as party symbols and flags (especially the red of PT) were declared unwelcome.

Over the course of the next 2 years, the wave of mobilization set off in June 2013 would undergo significant transformation. A moralistic anti-corruption agenda – already present in 2013, and according to which politicians and the political class are "all the same" and should be "kicked out" – came to overwhelm the protests. At the same time, the largest corruption investigations in the country's history got off the ground, revealing a massive graft scandal involving the state petroleum company, Petrobras. After PT's victory in the October 2014 general election, the demonstrations and widespread popular anger transformed into a phenomenon known as *antipetismo* (or anti-PT sentiment). The party – until 2005 widely seen as a principled, ethical force – came to be identified with the establishment, corruption and/or with the instrumentalization of the state for partisan interests. The most severe recession in Brazil's history, beginning in 2015, coupled with austerity measures designed to appease markets implemented by President Dilma Rousseff (PT), served to combust the political crisis.

By 2015, nationalist themes came to the fore, a consequence of middle- and upper-middle class leadership of the mobilizations. "My party is my country" became a common slogan, with protesters decked out in only the green and gold of the national flag. The greater force of this anti-partisanship was directed at the PT, and by extension the Left as a whole, because it was identified with politics as such. A new hero emerged in this period, Sergio Moro, the investigating judge in Operation Car Wash which targeted the illicit links between construction contractors, Petrobras and the political class. At the time, it felt as though the investigations might eviscerate the entirety of the political class. Two-thirds of Congress was under investigation for one illicit activity or another.

What might otherwise have been a proto-revolutionary situation instead began to look like a repeat of early 1990s Italy and the fall of the First Republic (see Chapter 6). In a country with a more recent history of rightist dictatorship, it might even presage a far more nefarious development. The right-wing street mobilizations called for the impeachment of Dilma Rousseff, who eventually succumbed to parliamentary machinations to remove her from office – a soft coup, in effect. The authority of the traditional establishment collapsed, while the Left remained fragmented and incapable of politicizing the situation in its favor. The PT stayed wedded to its strategy of class conciliation and compromise (post-politics) at a time when the bottom had fallen out of the political center, and the economic crisis meant the "everybody wins" moderation of the 2000s was unrealistic. The Radical Left, meanwhile, was too weak and fragmented to make hay, and was anyway demonized for being the most political force within politics – and therefore unpatriotic; a corrupting influence.[14]

By the 2018 elections, the traditional Center-Right found it had no traction, and all the dynamism rested with Jair Bolsonaro, a seven-term far-right law and order congressman who presented himself as an incorruptible outsider. The PT ran as moderate social democrats, promising a return to the good times of the boom years – i.e. the status quo ante – and lost.[15]

Of course, Brazil is hardly the linchpin of the global system and anyway has its own very particular history, with dynamics not generalizable to countries of the global North. Nevertheless, it offers us the most crystalline example of anti-politics – and in particular its anti-corruption variant. Brazil's case exemplifies the point repeated herein – that anti-corruption has two divergent tendencies. In one, it divests political representatives of credibility and legitimacy, urging a preponderant role for counter-majoritarian institution (for instance, putting unelected judges in charge, for they are seen as the only agents able to hold politicians to account – a process known as the judicialization of politics). Removing power from political representatives can also take the form of a neoliberal privatization agenda, whereby state intervention in the economy (including but not limited to state-owned enterprises (SOEs)) is seen as necessarily prone to corruption. Privatization is likely to go further than just selling off SOEs, as the capability of the state to provide services is also brought into question. The private provision of transportation, health and education are thus put on the menu. It is a tragic irony that combating the phenomenon of corruption (effectively, the privatization of politics) leads to greater privatization.

In the second tendency, a supposedly pure, undivided people emerges to fight a corrupt political class. So tainted is politics under the force of anti-corruption militancy that the divisions emanating from the political realm – parties, ideologies – come to be seen as corrupt too. However, instead of the people (or the working class) trusting itself and seizing power, a scenario of generalized distrust develops, in which all division must be smashed, so as to guarantee the ethical integrity of the nation.

Anti-corruption, as a form of anti-politics, thus leads to either post-politics (judicialization of politics, neoliberal technocracy) or to authoritarian, nationalist populism. Brazil's example shows that these two consequences can even coexist. Bolsonaro's nationalist rhetoric, repression of minorities and hatred of the Left is accompanied by neoliberal economic policies, the selling off of state assets to foreign interests and the glorification of the judiciary as agent of anti-corruption. At the social level, this finds reflection in the depoliticization and privatization of experience. If politics no longer offers any hope, best to seek refuge in family and faith, to defend that which is dear – with arms if need be.

The Left's unwillingness to thoroughly politicize, to break with a post-political status quo administered successfully by the

PT, led the inchoate revolt of June 2013 to its final denouement in the 2018 election of Jair Bolsonaro. Facile anti-politics, in its populist formulation ("the elites are all corrupt and in it for themselves, we the people are united in opposition") has repeatedly been seized upon by the Left over the past decade. It has borne no fruit, and in some cases, such as in Brazil, has led to disaster.

5.2 Horizontalism and participation

Growing inequality and precarity, and the breakdown of the neoliberal order, has led to repeated popular uprisings around the globe in the past decade – many of these exemplifying the second type of anti-politics from below. Bereft of properly ideological language – and the organizations and institutions that bear those specific ideas – crowds have expressed their indignation directly and nakedly against the authority of the political class, and sometimes the elite as a whole.

Before the 2019 uprisings mentioned at the start of the chapter, there was 2013. Recall that *The Economist* placed that year alongside the world-historic revolutions of 1848, 1968 and 1989 on its front cover in July 2013. But in contrast to those nineteenth- and twentieth-century events which the magazine held were restricted to Europe, 2013's revolts were supposedly taking place "Everywhere." Their essential characteristic was the anti-politics of "leaderlessness."

The return of "revolution" to general discourse happened even earlier, with the start of the Arab Spring in 2011. The modes of action and organizing, and the symbolism, of those revolts across the Middle East and North Africa set the template for uprisings in the first part of the decade. The taking of squares and setting up of encampments, organizing via social media, the V-for-Vendetta masks, the youthful energy and anti-political sloganeering...these all came to be repeated elsewhere. First at Occupy Wall Street, then in contexts as different as Spain,

Bulgaria, Brazil, Britain, Ukraine or Turkey. The political scientist Ivan Krastev remarked on the "strange kind of revolution" these uprisings represented.[16] They don't bear ideological labels, nor end up proposing new ideologies; even charismatic leaders are largely absent. They are remembered for their videos not manifestos – a very postmodern triumph of image over text.

Analyses that tried to sum up what drove these different protests generally foundered on the reality of hugely divergent contexts, compositions, aims and outcomes. Protests expressed no particular belief in capitalism, but they were certainly not socialist. Some saw the events as an uprising of the "global middle class," but that raises more problems than it solves – many were significantly proletarian in composition, only deemed "middle class" because the protesters were better educated and had iPhones. Almost universally, the protests were in favor of democracy, but at the same time eschewed representation of any kind. "The closest the revolutionaries have come in making a sociological argument is when they denounce the blood-sucking elites of the 1 percent. The government, meanwhile, is simply a conspiracy in power that can be opposed but not really understood."[17] The global protests of the early 2010s – and many in the late 2010s – were above all about *participation without representation*.

The disappointments of Occupy, and the mode of organization of which it is the clearest exemplar, have been endlessly discussed. Similarly, many have noted its precedents in Argentina's anti-neoliberal revolt of 2001, under the impact of its debt crisis. There, neighborhood assemblies and factory occupations emphasized *horizontalidad*, and exclaimed ¡*Que se vayan todos!* (all of them must go!). Nevertheless, it is worth here restating what made *horizontalidad* appealing.

The demonstrations' anti-politics inheres in their emphasis on decision-making by consensus, the rejection of all hierarchies, glorification of leaderlessness and the valorization of participation for its own sake. The loose structures and their open-ended nature allow protests to expand quickly, drawing in new crowds and different sections of societies, each individual bringing with them their own grievances and hopes. The lack of coherence around a determinate ideological orientation – and in many cases, even the absence of clear political demands – make them a free-for-all. The experience of being there, "doing something," giving voice to one's frustrations became their most important aspect. That, combined with the sharing of images, led to them being criticized as narcissistic protests, more about "you" and "your feelings" than the achievement of political ends.

What is now clear is that what made these horizontalist free-for-all protests capable of expanding into mass demonstrations is exactly what guaranteed their failure. Nearly all these uprisings, when unable to overcome their anti-politics, met one of four ends. In the first scenario, the movements evaporated once initial energies were spent. The lack of formal organization meant there was no durable agency to sustain mobilization, and that absence meant any new ideas that the movements threw up found no concrete embodiment. The Gilets Jaunes set fire to France for a year (November 2018 to late 2019), but eventually petered-out. Alternatively, these movements were defeated, the force of repression dispersing crowds, as happened in Turkey. In a third case, they were co-opted, as the most anti-political strands of the movement were seized upon by more powerful forces – as exemplified by Brazil. Or, fourthly, and most tragically, they result in civil war – for which, see Syria or Ukraine.

None of this is to make an argument for charismatic leadership, or insertion into the formal politics of the state, or hierarchies per se, nor is it to diminish the importance of participation. The point is rather to warn of the dangers of an anti-politics that rejects division, representation and political authority. If popular movements from below are to succeed in taking power, it is indispensable to create formal representative structures. The masses may come out onto the streets in anger, but a pure, direct democracy is unsustainable. The psychic rewards from participation – "feeling part of something" – may be universal, but that does not mean everyone wants to tend to organizational minutiae constantly. The working class still has to go to work.

The more politicized strata who preach horizontalism also engage in abnegating their own authority. Instead of making a play for leadership of a movement, proposing ideas and letting these be openly contested, horizontalists hide behind a hyper-democratic facade of consensus and constant participation.

This horizontalist period, however, seems to have been left behind. The year 2011 was one of the key moments of emergence out of the End of History. People were back on the streets and, suddenly, it felt as if the future was not taken for granted but once again open – or at least slightly ajar. But such was the effect of depoliticization over the preceding period that people brought with them into the new era the same self-defeating mindset. The anti-globalization movement of the late 1990s/early 2000s preached changing the world without taking power, and this same attitude came to be replicated in Occupy and various other movements. Decline of trust in formal politics continued apace, but no new ideology emerged to overthrow the state, or even the status quo. Instead what we got was raw indignation, coupled with a recoil from politics itself.

This may all feel like a thing of the past, especially in the global North. The failures of horizontalism prompted a re-acquaintance with power and representation. The movements of the squares in Spain and Greece bred Podemos and Syriza. Newly politicized Millennials regrouped around Bernie Sanders' campaign for president and Corbynism in the UK. But the defeat of left-populism prompts the question: will disappointment cleave left currents away from formal organizations, from political parties, once again?

5.3 Revolutionism

Where the horizontalists mistrusted political authority to such a degree they failed to organize for power, the left-wing re-encounter with formal politics led to an embrace of electoralism and reformism. Of course, it was not the contesting of elections and fighting for reforms that doomed left-populism. Rather, it was the failure to break with political institutions (the EU in the case of Corbyn's Labour and Syriza; the Democratic Party in Bernie Sanders' movement).

In response to these conundrums, there is a strain of radical thought that eschews "politics" (in the sense of the formal institutions of the state) in favor of "the social" – especially social insurrection. Although marginal on the Left today, this tendency starts from the presupposition that all engagement in state structures – including trying to take state power – will lead to co-optation and moderation, whereby "the political" would come to dominate "the social." This counter-position of the social to the political is based on a reading of Marx according to which, for example, the declarations of liberty, equality, fraternity are merely political masks to obscure the reality of exploitation at the social level. Rather than seek to realize those values within existing institutions (reformism), the point would be to overthrow those institutions and transform social relations, ushering in an era of true freedom.

What this perspective ignores is the ill-health of "the social" today. The trends already explored in this book – depoliticization, lack of trust in institutions, social disorganization and declining civic participation – afflict grassroots organizations too, be they trade unions, workers' parties or social movements. The revolutionist desire for the overthrow of the political ends up being, in today's conditions, an insurrectionary rather than a revolutionary proposal. We thus come full circle, back to anti-politics.

This tendency can be illustrated through the concrete example of Brexit. The radical argument for British exit from the EU was based on the idea of rupture from a post-political institution that sought to foreclose politics. The EU influences political relations within the nation-state, just as much as it manages relations between them. Rupture would, firstly, return power to national parliaments – more representative than EU institutions – and, secondly, provoke further democratizing reform within nation-states, once the buttress of the depoliticizing EU was removed.

For the revolutionists, the idea of a "more democratic" national parliament was just more reformist nonsense, an attempt to ennoble bourgeois institutions and encase politics in the defunct nation-state. In the presence of a militant and organized revolutionary working-class movement, such a position might be realistic and intensely political. In our circumstances, it can only be a disempowering dead-end which abandons the task of democratizing society and the state in favor of an eschatological final event that would emerge *ex nihilo*.[18]

The point here is not to dismiss revolution. Rather, it is that the low levels of even basic trade union militancy, let alone revolutionary movements, mean the horizon of revolution has drifted from view. The challenge today is to be neither naive nor cynical. Those who know too little act as if parliamentary democracy could lead to socialism, if only the right coalition could be cobbled together, if only an electoral 51 percent were achieved. That is to forget so many lessons of the past in which this has failed. Indeed, those past failures were at least backed-up by a higher degree of social organization than today. The cynical path is, perhaps, to know too much. In the consciousness of these failures, one decides that all participation in formal politics is doomed, and that society should not involve itself in politics. Radical politicization needs to navigate between the precipices of cynicism and naivety.

5.4 Left defeatism

The failure of horizontalist "people power" movements in the first half of the 2010s followed by the defeat of left-populism in the second half has bred defeatism. Faced with repeated populist breakthroughs across Europe, but unable to wield populism to its own electoral ends, the Left has in some cases returned to the defeatist attitude that held throughout the End of History. In Britain, the combined effect of Brexit and the resounding defeat of Corbyn's Labour at the polls in late 2019 led to a sadly predictable reaction: the liberal-left wrote-off the masses as hopelessly reactionary, or at least brainwashed by the conservative media.

Already in 2017, Eliane Glaser, cited in Chapter 3 as an ostensible opponent of anti-politics, declared that, due to Brexit:

> it was abruptly clear that direct democracy is not necessarily better at all; that majoritarianism has inherent problems that we didn't really anticipate, because – as with the vast majority of commentators blindsided by right-wing populism – everyone was assuming that we just needed to give people more power, and everything would be okay. It's not necessarily a more progressive situation if more people vote and they are mostly right-wing and "the will of the people" equates to enabling exploitation and disempowerment.[19]

The specter of majoritarianism, instead of being a terror for the establishment and inspiration for the Left, ends up spooking both. The institutional Left's vaunting of the 99 percent or "the many," the insistence on the corruption of existing institutions, the need for rupture and the end of neoliberalism...these are all shown to be empty words. Recourse then is had to various *dei ex machina* to save the Left. The Covid-19 crisis is but the latest such instance.[20]

Demographic changes are a favored escape. Confronted

with the knowledge that the under-35s voted overwhelmingly for Labour in the UK, or Generation Z's positive appraisal of "socialism" in the US, or the German Green's plurality support among under-25s, the institutional Left pins its hopes on the dying-off of older generations to create its required demographic majority. An alternative version sees ethnicity rather than generational politics pushing us toward demographic destiny. In the US, the relative shrinking of the white majority and growth in Latino constituencies leads to the belief that a "blue wave" is just around the corner.

Needless to say, this is no guarantee of success: the young, when they age, are fully capable of conservatism, Latinos of any age likewise. More importantly, it abandons politicization to the whims of objective factors, and ones not even directly related to class. Rather than try to raise people's consciousness about the way the world works, about the immanent power workers have (but fail to exercise), they rely on the slow progress of time to do its job. The Left that emerged in the period between the GFC and the Covid-19 crisis adopted post-political strategies of putting people in boxes, marketing segments, that grow or shrink due to impersonal factors. No arguments are won, no workers are organized, and class is abandoned in favor of generational or ethnic identity.

A related escape is to hunker down in left subculture. In this guise, leftists retreat to strongholds in metropolitan urban cores, defensively trying to maintain the integrity of an ethical core. A coalition of university graduates and some members of the multi-ethnic working class then finds itself unable to broaden out to the working class in depressed regions. The story is the same in the US, in Britain and in much of Western Europe. This approach divides the working class along quasi-moral lines – those that continue to vote for the institutional Left (the good ones) and those swayed by right-wing populism (the bad ones). This is merely another form of identity politics, but instead of markers of ascribed characteristics (race, gender, etc.), politico-cultural ones are adopted in their place. It is precisely *anti*-political because, instead of the universalizing drive of politicization, we find a logic of culture wars. According to this line of thinking, camps are arrayed on two sides, with tastes, habits, backgrounds and political preferences all aligned. Rather than be united in class struggle, with its capacity of overcoming individual and group differences, differences take precedence.[21]

5.5 Anti-politics from above

The emergence of widespread anti-political sentiment has created an opportunity for anti-politicians to wield this anger to their benefit. Most often, this attempt is known as populism. It is a weapon available both to traditional political elites as well as new, rising ones.

In the UK, where Brexit threatened – but ultimately failed – to dethrone the political class, more traditional elites have benefited. Already in June 2016, the Conservative Justice Secretary Michael Gove – an MP since 2005 and repeated shadow cabinet and cabinet minister – was challenged to name economists who were in favor of withdrawal from the EU. Refusing to do so, he declared, "people in this country have had enough of experts." More than just an opportunist tactic seized on at the moment, this approach would come to inform Boris Johnson's shocking victory in December 2019.

Faced with anger over the Brexit impasse – and confronted by a Labour Party that failed fully to commit to seeing through the referendum result, before fatally positioning itself in favor of a second referendum – Johnson's Conservatives managed historic victories in the Labour heartlands of declining post-industrial northern and midlands constituencies. Allied to promises of greater state spending, the Tories' promise to "get Brexit done" was at once an act of seizing the populist revolt around Brexit, while at the same time a means of defusing its potential (an act of post-politics). Wrongly characterized as a British Trump, the patrician Boris Johnson is no anti-politician. Instead, his revamped One-Nation Conservatism represents an attempt to capture anti-political energies (frustration and exhaustion with Brexit and, by extension, the entire political class) for electoral gain, while providing the foundations for the relegitimation of the British political class. Getting Brexit done would thus contain an explosive situation.

Elsewhere, anti-politicians have emerged from less traditional backgrounds and presented more serious challenges to political establishments, all the while leaving the operations of neoliberal capitalism very much in place. It is remarkable how many contemporary "populist" leaders come from culturally peripheral backgrounds, rather than the traditional milieus of the political elite – though rarely from the working class itself.

Jair Bolsonaro may have been a congressman for seven straight terms before becoming president, but his political origins are as an army captain whose positions proved too radically right-wing even for the anti-communist Brazilian military establishment. Bolsonaro was raised in a small town, the son of an unlicensed dentist – not salt of the earth, but a far cry from the backgrounds of Brazil's traditional political elite. Viktor Orban was born into a middle-class family in a small and poor rural town in which books and newspapers were hardly read. A liberal initially, his encounter with the traditional Budapest intelligentsia was a negative one. The literati were condescending to the rube Orban, an experience that provoked his break with liberalism. Recep Tayyip Erdogan is the son of a Turkish Coast Guard captain who split his childhood between a poor neighborhood of Istanbul and a distant provincial town on the Black Sea coast. Unlike the traditionally secular Istanbul intellectual and political elite, Erdogan had attended a religious vocational high school, and always used his religious conservatism to appeal to the provinces.

To the extent these leaders are able to sell their personal

biographies as testament to their outsider status, it is because of a cultural alterity rather than a class-based one. They are middle class, but rarely come from the capital or metropolis, they are never scions of political, cultural or intellectual elites, and often bear more conservative cultural attitudes than the latter. This formative experience is the cornerstone of their popular appeal, whatever else they may say and do. Though ascension into the economic elite is a distant prospect for many, becoming part of the cultural elite is perhaps even less fathomable – especially in the provinces (one might, just maybe, become a millionaire but "fitting in" is another story). That sense of exclusion can provide the raw material for an anti-political proposition: "I too am an uncouth outsider, who uses raw language, refuses to follow established codes, and am unbound by the strictures of traditional politics."

It is for this reason that left-wing protestations that, "these are not really outsiders, they defend powerful economic interests," however true, often fall flat. Yes, right-wing populism is generally not anti-systemic. Nor are right-wing populists able to depend upon majority working-class support in many cases. But they are able to capture sections of that class because of their oppositional stance with respect to the traditional political elites. Meanwhile, much of the Left continues to be identified with cultural elites, and so struggles to speak to and shape anti-political energies.

Indeed, it is this last fact that explains why it is left-liberals who attract the greatest populist ire. That ideological grouping is the most wedded to the formal codes of politics, to the media as an institution, to the legal apparatus of the state, and above all to providing secular moral guidance to society. Right-liberals (or neoliberals) are far more cynical, wedded only to the market. That explains why they are less frequently targeted by anti-politics (because they are relatively apolitical). It is also, at root, why neoliberals readily ally with, or tolerate, right-populists:

neither presents a mortal threat to the other's authority. And so a counter-elite might take charge of government, but nothing substantially changes.

5.6 Too left, too populist

Anti-politics, then, continues to encounter dead ends. We do not live in an age of masses. If we did, the long-term crumbling of party systems in Western liberal democracies – and the more recent breakdown of the neoliberal order – would meet insurrection. Anti-politics might become revolutionary overthrow.

In the absence of mass participation, anti-politics from below has a pop-up character. Protests sprout, tweets are sent, new movements are christened...and then evaporate. Energies may then be absorbed by other forces. Post-political technocracy may seek to displace corrupt politicians with judges. Authoritarian nationalists may point the finger at partisanship or liberal civil society, with crackdowns quickly following. Either way, anti-political revolts, denouncing the bankruptcy of the political class, terminate in yet another political closure. The "void" between society and state is papered over.

Left-populist attempts have also failed – they have proved at once too left and too populist.[22] Too closely associated with "the Left" to properly incorporate different segments of the population, they have not been able to benefit from the breakdown of the party systems that have been hegemonic since the end of the Second World War. Meanwhile, they also proved too populist: they resisted the formalization of organizations and structures to act as conduits for the popular will. Moreover, in resisting traditional ideological-class alignment, they have proved fissiparous. And while cases vary country to country (Greece saw genuine mass mobilization, which guided Syriza to power), the continuing domination of left-populist attempts by professional-managerial class activists and leadership has seen that section of society's worldviews and interests prevail.

Anti-politics is not going away. It emerged and then flourished in a post-ideological age in which long-term declines in trust in political institutions came to a head. The strains of the breakdown of the neoliberal order and growing inequality breed anger and frustration. In consequence, rejection of the current order attaches itself to the most visible holders of power and authority: the political class.

Political establishments and the sections of the middle class who have benefited from and accommodated themselves to the End of History then rush to defend "politics." The term is thus further besmirched through the association of "politics" with hollow and undemocratic "post-politics." This breeds yet angrier reactions. To break out of this cycle, popular movements must come to terms with representation and political authority. Indeed, the rejection of a political elite that denies its own authority, that remains in charge but pretends not to be, should be a prompt for the masses to seize the mantle of political authority themselves.

Chapter 6

Italy: Country of the Future

Italy did not so much creep into the End of History as tumble-in head first. At the end of the Cold War, domestic and regional events combined to break-up the arrangements that had been built up in Italy since the end of the Second World War. Nowhere in the world was the transition into the End of History more abrupt – if one discounts the societies where really existing socialism collapsed overnight – than on the Italian peninsula.

In 1991, the Italian Communist Party decided it would disband, and become the Democratic Party of the Left (PDS). It had once been the largest communist party in the West, peaking at 2.3 million members after the end of the Second World War and achieving over a third of the share of votes in the mid-1970s. Even at its dissolution, it retained nearly 1 million members. Suddenly, the Christian Democrats, who had ruled Italy almost without interruption throughout the First Republic (1948-1992), had lost their raison d'être – anticommunism.

Italy now wished to become a "normal country." No more communism, terrorism, mafia, corruption, or disorder. This also meant a change to Italy's economic model. Prior to the age of globalization, Italy had one of the most interventionist states in the West, with large sections of the economy controlled by the state conglomerate IRI. It was initially set up under fascism and played an important role in Italy's postwar boom, compensating for the lack of a reliable big bourgeoisie in a country dominated by small family firms. One important step in making this change was to join the European Monetary Union. In order for this to happen, it had to meet the Convergence Criteria stipulated at Maastricht in 1992. Low inflation, low interest rates, a stable currency, a limited budget deficit and reduced national debt were the commandments handed down. Italy only had one course of action available: cuts to public expenditure and flexibilization of labour markets. Italy was disciplined to the requirements of globalization, as mediated by European regional integration.

As with other European countries at the time, Italian society was becoming increasingly commercialized, following the American model. Privatized consumerism boomed and visual culture superseded the written word. Television, previously limited to tedious programming on the RAI, the state broadcaster, suddenly had private competitors purveying much glitzier fare. Behind this development was a former real estate mogul whose business empire now included advertising, newspapers, publishing and football, as well as TV: Silvio Berlusconi. His stated aim was to bring entertainment, advertising and consumer goods into people's homes.[1]

In 1992, some Milan-based magistrates began to investigate political corruption in the center-left Italian Socialist Party. The investigation was led by a crusading section of the judiciary who aimed to clean up politics for good and who saw themselves as the moral heart of Italy, as against the unscrupulous capital of much of the bourgeoisie and its accomplices in politics. Soon the investigation – dubbed "*Mani Pulite*" (Clean Hands) – would broaden out spectacularly, uncovering a corrupt system that came to be called *Tangentopoli*, or "bribesville." It led to the fall of numerous industrialists and politicians from the Right to the Center-Left, many of whom were arrested, charged and sentenced. The powerful head of the Socialist Party and friend of Berlusconi, Bettino Craxi, would eventually go into exile in Tunisia instead of face charges. By the end of Clean Hands, the investigations returned not-guilty verdicts in a mere 14 percent of cases. It is hard to overstate what a bombshell the anti-corruption crusade was.

Things moved fast. In 1993 Italy gained its first ever – but hardly its last – government of technical experts. By the 1994 elections, all the main parties that had composed that technocratic government had been dissolved. Of the largest parties, only the former Communists in their new form – the PDS – remained intact. With outrage over corruption still roiling, they looked set to win the 1994 elections.

But in the final stretch, a brand-new party, formed and launched with the aid of the most advanced political marketing techniques of the day, swept to power in an improbable right-wing coalition. Silvio Berlusconi became prime minister as the head of his newly-minted *Forza Italia* party, with the aid of a post-fascist party that still publicly idolized Mussolini (the National Alliance) and a northern Italy-based separatist party which pushed xenophobia, racism, anti-corruption and hatred of the political establishment in Rome (Lega Nord).

The hugely popular anti-corruption campaign led by the crusading judiciary did not manage, however, to re-moralize the republic in the way it had wanted. Nor did it break the cozy business-politics nexus that had become a feature of Italian capitalism and which, until then, no one had dared touch, lest it hand the Italian state to the Communists on a plate. What happened instead was a political vacuum where the mass parties of the Christian Democrats and the Socialist Party once stood, one which would be filled by a charismatic billionaire media mogul, a one-man business-politics nexus. Though the government elected in 1994 would shortly fall, Berlusconi would dominate the following decades in a way no single individual ever had in Italy.

Berlusconi's party was a novel creation. Its name (approved by focus group) was a football chant ('Let's go Italy!'). The organization was cooked-up in swish meeting rooms as an electoral vehicle for its leader. Fifty of the party's parliamentarians when it first entered the legislature were employees of Publitalia, the advertising arm of Mediaset, the media company owned by Berlusconi. There was no internal party democracy nor any grassroots; it existed purely for TV. This was not a political party as we knew it. It was a "business party" or "party-as-firm." Its coherence was exclusively dependent on the charismatic figure at its top. "We *Forza Italia* deputies have not got a leader, but a boss," explained a former parliamentarian who joined the party because it seemed to offer a modernized Christian Democracy, only to turn critic later on.[2]

Berlusconi's first government fell after only a few months, prompted by the disgruntlement of coalition partner Lega Nord. In a moment emblematic of the times, the main forces from across the political spectrum (the populist and separatist Lega, the center-left PDS and the former Christian Democrats of the Popular Party) made a pact to avoid new elections and put a technocratic government in place which could, among other objectives, pass cuts to pensions.[3] For the former communists, in particular, this moment proved symbolic, as the Center-Left (as it was now called) started its drift toward the neoliberal Center-Right, rallying under the banners of rationalization, reducing bureaucracy and cleaning up government.

The technical cabinet formed then would remain in power until the 1996 elections, which the Center-Left won. Led by Romano Prodi – nicknamed *Il Professore* and an economics professor, as well as Goldman Sachs advisor and later President of the European Commission – the Olive Tree coalition would rule until 2001. By that time, Forza Italia had grown to 300,000 members, but that did not mean it was a democratic, mass party. It had no fixed decision-making processes and its regional heads were appointed by the man at the top. Berlusconi returned to power in 2001 and ruled until 2013, making him Italy's longest-serving postwar prime minister. During this time, his party would not become more organic or democratic. Indeed, in 2007, Forza Italia changed name to Popolo della Libertà ("People of Freedom"), without any consultation of members and affiliates.

So, if citizens were now to be passive recipients of politics, rather than active participants, what is it they were receiving? Or better put, what was Berlusconi selling? On face value, it was *liberty*, as his various electoral vehicles repeatedly emphasized (the Pole of Liberties, the House of Liberties, the People of Liberty). But this was an exclusively negative liberty, the freedom to be left alone, to pursue consumer pleasures and to be absolved of any civic responsibilities. It was explicitly anti-Left, but it also distinguished itself from the old traditionalist Right, refocusing around modernity, efficiency and dynamism. This appealed to a section of society that could be called the entrepreneurial middle class, whose aims were market reforms and liberalization, and who wanted to have the state weigh less heavily on their lives.

Italy's large number of small businesses, family firms and family shops provided the social base, for whom the tax state was an antagonist. Berlusconi's typically neoliberal emphasis on the private over the public and the flexible over the inflexible (or bureaucratic) chimed with this middle class. He also railed against the judiciary, for although he profited from the anti-corruption campaign's evisceration of the old political class, Berlusconi played to a popular appreciation for rule-bending. The small business owner might hate graft between politicians and big business, but he also needed to get by; overly officious inspectors were an impediment to his freedom too.

Berlusconi, though, did not just present one face, that of the dynamic, modern businessman pursuing pro-market policies. There was also a large degree of patrimonialism – that is, when political administration "is treated as a purely personal affair of the ruler, and political power is considered part of his personal property, which can be exploited by means of contributions and fees."[4] Berlusconi was a media mogul who leveraged his business empire into politics. The pillars of his administration were his personal authority and charisma, the acquisitive ambitions that fueled his empire's growth, the arbitrary whims of the man as patron, and the reciprocity of favors.[5]

The temptation to perceive these elements through stereotypes of Italian Mafiosi should be resisted. The apposite comparison is to a man like Michael Bloomberg in the US, or Thaksin Shinawatra in Thailand, both mega-rich businessmen turned politicians. Indeed, this was the age of media moguls. Rupert Murdoch in the Anglophone world or Roberto Marinho and his heirs in Brazil are comparable figures, with the difference that they sought to rule only indirectly. In fact, France's Bernard Tapie – business mogul, TV entertainer, football club owner and politician – would be the most accurate comparison, though the French justice system would interrupt Tapie's career. One can wonder what might have been of France should Tapie have continued his ascent.

While patrimonialism is self-evidently a corruption of democracy, it is important to recall that this was all sold as a new politics, one of novelty, success and efficiency, against the old corrupt establishment. The Center-Left proved unable to get a foothold, bar two brief interruptions to Berlusconi's rule in which Romano Prodi formed a government. The Center-Left found itself in a contradiction. It could not fundamentally challenge the neoliberal precepts of the new politics, because it had gone along with them. Instead, it focused on Berlusconi's crassness and impropriety.

The Center-Left's political base at this time was what might be called the "civic middle class." It was from this section of society that *Il Cavaliere* drew most opposition. They advocated in defense of rationality and republican virtues, defending the public realm from private interests. Street protest, such as that in 2002 when hundreds of thousands took to the streets wearing Pinocchio noses in mockery of the prime minister, mobilized public sector workers, students and the professional middle class. The banners of opposition – defense of the judiciary and public institutions, as well as of democracy, responsible consumption and civic values – would never succeed in toppling Berlusconi over the course of his terms in office.

This may well have been because Berlusconi's electoral success was based not only on neoliberal managerialism or on old clientelistic relations, but a specific and new kind of populism. His was a specifically personalized style of rule, rooted in his image as a successful businessman, a showman and an everyman – all at the same time. Television was essential to this projection, a medium capable of erasing boundaries between reality and dreams. Here was politics using the tools of celebrity culture: figures whom you do not know personally and yet to whom you feel intimately attached; the celebrity is at once superhuman and ordinary.

The personalization of politics allowed Berlusconi to appear dynamic and decisive, a man with solutions. Notably, in 2011, when many thousands of migrants from Africa were landing on the Italian island of Lampedusa each month, Berlusconi declared, "I promise, within three days, there will not be any immigrants left on this island." He added, in a supposed show of seriousness of intent and confidence in his own success, that he had just bought a house on the island himself.[6]

Popular trust in Berlusconi was not "political" in any traditional sense. It was not loyalty based on allegiance to an ideology or to the practice of political values. In fact, there was relatively little reference in his discourse toward either values of the Left (solidarity, welfare) or the Right (order, national identity, tradition). Instead, this was an anti-politics of the everyday. Berlusconi projected notions of immediate self-interest, success, permissive fun and enjoyment. His audience was alleviated of traditional civic responsibilities, while his impropriety and display of prejudices was, rather than a shortcoming, more evidence that he was just like you and me. Even his legal transgressions could be understood as permission-giving: you too have "special liberty."[7]

In Italy's new republic, old loyalties had vanished. The

two cultures which had dominated Italian life for decades – one Communist, one Catholic – each with their sets of local organizations, institutions and political parties, were no more. What these cultures had shared was a sense of social solidarity, expressed either in the form of welfare or charity. In their wake went culturally conservative attitudes; in came individualism. In this increasingly passive and atomized "audience democracy,"[8] in which Italians trusted their political institutions little, politics came to be mediated by television. And that meant only one winner because, as historian Paul Ginsborg starkly put it, "television is Berlusconi."[9] While the Center-Left rallied behind increasingly discredited and untrusted institutions – and the civic virtues they demanded of citizens – Berlusconi instead simply said: "you may."

Until the early 2000s, it was plausible to ask whether *Il Cavaliere* would prove to be a prototype or merely an exception. By 2011, one study of the new style of politics inaugurated by Berlusconi concluded that he was indeed a prototype.[10] Possibly earlier than any other politician – or at any rate more decisively – Berlusconi synthesized this new politics. Former German chancellor Gerhard Schroeder, former US president Bill Clinton, US 1992 presidential candidate Ross Perot, former UK prime minister Tony Blair, former governor of California Arnold Schwarzenegger, murdered Dutch populist Pim Fortuyn, former French president Nicolas Sarkozy – all these could be said to embody the celebrity, personalization and commodification of politics put on show in Italy at the End of History. But none condensed so many crucial features in one person and political project.

The start-up party run on the model of a business, the use of TV and celebrity politics, the simultaneous appropriation of anti-corruption and corruption, the anti-politics of the everyday, the projection of business success as a key attribute, all are resumed in Berlusconi's project. Moreover, populism had become, not just in Italy but across consolidated democracies, "the hegemonic form of democratic politics itself."[11]

In fact, it was not just Berlusconi who was the prototype for the politics of the End of History. It was Italy itself. Or if "prototype" suggests too much in the way of conscious design, then maybe Italy was an *augury* (suitably Roman in origin). Italy foretold the future of "advanced democracies" in the End of History.

The breakdown of the old politics of the postwar era was particularly abrupt in Italy, under the force of Mani Pulite. The decomposition of historic blocs of Right and Left was rapid. If contemporary national politics across Europe today is marked by the vote share of the Center-Left and Center-Right blocs dipping below 50 percent, where previously they accounted for an immense majority, then it was in Italy where the old arrangements came apart earliest and quickest. What took their place was an institutional politics cut off from mass participation. Already in 1997, one scholar described the Italian state as "hollow with a hard shell": hollow, because civil society struggled to have its interest represented by the state; hard, because the state's capacities in areas like immigration or law and order remain, and indeed had been strengthened.[12] At the level of ideas, too, politics was no longer divided on ideological and class lines, but debated around "shared" objectives of rationalization and efficiency, of preparing Italy to compete on the European and global market. The new politics of anti-corruption got its first airing in Italy, with the sight of the powerful being arrested becoming a moralized spectacle. The practice of "lawfare" – the use of corruption allegations to pursue political ends – was also trialed here before renditions elsewhere. Indeed, well before Trump started chanting "lock her up," this model of spectacular anti-corruption politics had its tragic re-enactment in Brazil from 2014-18, following the Italian script verbatim.[13]

Italy's desire to become a "normal country," to modernize

according to what it envied in countries to its north, ended up coinciding with the loss of its future. The country has stagnated for 2 decades. Economic growth has flatlined since 2000, and its GDP per capita is slightly lower today than 20 years ago. Low fertility rates and emigration of the young has meant the number of Italian citizens living in Italy has fallen to 55 million for the first time in 90 years. Italy now trades on the inheritance of its past; it is a living museum.

Anxieties over decline, especially in demographic terms, may be a factor in the country's hostility to immigration. Surveys regularly show the country toward the bottom of the table in terms of positive attitudes toward immigrants, alongside countries like Greece and Hungary – both of which also have low birth rates and high rates of emigration. This has provided xenophobic forces with the raw material to advance racist politics. And locked into the Eurozone as it is, burdened by high levels of debt, the country has no institutional avenues to break free of its historic funk.

Economic stagnation and demographic decline are very much a European story today. But in Italy, these trends were present much earlier, as were their political consequences. The Lega Nord first came into government with Berlusconi, in 1994, purveying a xenophobic and anti-political populism. That it found itself in government yet again in 2018 should not have been a historic shock. Indeed, in the interim, Italy has even seen a populism of the Center-Left, in Matteo Renzi's attempt to make the Democratic Party "leader-centered" (indeed, Renzi was described as a "Berlusconi of the Left"). There has also been the rise of a "pure" populist party in the form of the Five Star Movement, which would form a government in 2018 with the Lega (by then no longer a regionalist party). In the end, it was an appropriate historical irony that Berlusconi's attempt to run as an *anti-populist* in 2018 found little support. Having first laid the ground for formal politics as a whole to be carried out in a populist register, he found himself outflanked 25 years later.[14]

A final dimension to the Italian augury of the End of History is found in an internal, structural relation: the country's North-South divide. The acceptance of this historic inequality as a permanent reality signaled the end of the developmental state and its replacement by a neoliberal one. Moreover, it places Italy in an ambiguous position with regard to the European "core" of countries like Germany and the Netherlands. Italy, from the beginning a central member of European integration efforts, is now seen as part of the European periphery, despite its North arguably belonging to the advanced European core. The country may be disparaged as home to patrimonialism, clientelism, corruption and general backwardness in politics, economy and society – but these are the same terms with which the country's North disparages its South. There is even a word for this: "mezzogiornification" (after the *Mezzogiorno*, the Italian South), meaning the process by which regions or countries become economically backward and dependent in relation to richer, more industrialized ones. So, contained within Italy is a contradiction – core and periphery – that plays out across the European continent, and indeed the world.

But once again, Italy shows itself to be the country of the future. The North-South divide increasingly finds an echo in regional disparities in other nation-states. See, for example, the role it played in Brexit or in Trump's election. And mirror images are found in other areas too. Backward political practices such as patrimonialism, in which political authority is extended through interpersonal relations, and clientelism, in which loyalty to the leadership is given in return for protection and favors, appear to have infiltrated "modern" politics. The Bolsonaro administration's dependence on personal loyalty, exemplified by the president's deployment of his sons and the appointment of far-right cranks to ministerial positions, could be dismissed as the backwardness of a country on capitalism's semi-periphery.

But the same could not be said for the global hegemon, where Trump relies on his family and his hangers-on to fill key positions. This confusion of private and public interests, and the running of the administration as some sort of household, is a clear sign of degeneration.

In advanced democracies, the establishment always made a great effort to preserve the illusion of the state's neutrality. But is that now coming into question? We increasingly see factions of the ruling class assault the state, trying to use it to partisan ends, with consequences like the politicization of the judiciary. Is the Democratic Party's alliance with the deep state and Robert Mueller's investigation of Donald Trump not just such a case? And is this not just another example of the *Italianification* of politics? So construction magnate and "Mr Television" Silvio Berlusconi anticipated construction magnate and "Mr Television" Donald Trump.

If foretelling the growing disorganization of establishment politics and the institutionalization of populism were not enough, Italy had a final tale to tell. At the very end of the End of History, it became the first Western country to face a massive coronavirus outbreak. The UK, the US and others were slow to react, ignoring that the cataclysmic events in Italy were coming for them too. The ensuing economic crisis in Italy was the worst in Europe, strangling an already limp economy burdened by debt, high unemployment and low productivity. The small businesses that make up a large chunk of the Italian economy suffered badly, presaging the increasing concentration of capital across the West, as huge corporations swallowed up the minnows. The drop in confidence in European institutions was precipitous. Might Italy be the first to leave the Eurozone, yet another Italian augury?

Chapter 7

The Shapes Don't Fit: Parties, Protest, Class and Culture

The decline of mass politics still disfigures our age. Yet many act as if politics is broadly the same as it always was. Of course, we recognize certain transformations that have occurred: media have changed – less face-to-face, more digital; the ideological spectrum has shifted – rightwards since the 1980s; we talk about "Overton windows" – neoliberal breakdown has opened up previously forgotten possibilities...

What the metaphors of shifting and opening/closing miss is an arguably more important phenomenon: hollowness. Our political world has retained its external appearance, but if you crack open the shell, there's nothing inside. We still have parties and elections and campaigns. We occasionally have big protests. Even trade unions still have some members (quite a lot if you live in a Nordic country or Belgium). Yet the reality is that party membership has declined, electoral participation has decreased and union density is much diminished. There is a void where "the people" should be.

During the End of History, none of this seemed to matter much. After all, we were meant to have left behind all those tensions and passions of mass politics. The return of politics has not quite filled the void. What *has* happened is that new and sometimes strange political forms have emerged that try to answer popular desires for participation – to be active subjects, not just passive objects of politics. Or even just simply to be heard: *we're still here*.

In this chapter, we will revisit the ways in which mass politics fell into decay, focusing on parties, elections, unions and other civic organizations. Then we will explore how the return of politics has led to novel party forms that sought to capture the new will to participate and shape society. The resurgence of the Labour Party under Jeremy Corbyn, the return of the DSA, and the popular impulse behind Podemos and Syriza all seemed to embody new possibilities for Left politics.

After this we will turn to informal types of participation, in particular mass protest. Despite feverish claims over the past decade about the revolt of the youth, protest actually never went away during the End of History. Often the young and middle class took to the streets, in lieu of other forms of engagement. This suggests a change in the class composition of left-wing politics. One of its effects has been to re-energize culture wars. So we ponder a difficult question: what if instead of the return of politics, the passions that have recently been unleashed lead merely to the return of head-banging culture wars?

7.1 End of the party

The era of the End of History saw the full unfolding of long-term dynamics: the end of party government and its modes of popular sovereignty.[1] Although the old vehicles remained – often, such as in Germany, the UK and the US, under the very same names – the 1990s and 2000s saw parties divest themselves of their substantive function of organizing social conflict and structuring political division. They became more appendages of the state – "cartel parties" in political scientist Peter Mair's terminology – than organic social institutions.[2] As the late Mair concluded: "The age of party democracy has passed. Although the parties themselves remain, they have become so disconnected from the wider society, and pursue a form of competition that is so lacking in meaning, that they no longer seem capable of sustaining democracy in its present form."[3] We arrived at the End of the End of History, then, with hollowed-out and disintegrated political parties.

Political parties' inability and unwillingness to channel

popular frustrations led to the anti-politics described in Chapter 5. But these dynamics have also generated new vehicles that have looked to address the distance between "politics" and "the people." Two notable examples are Podemos in Spain and the Five Star Movement (M5S) in Italy, parties whose "populist" elements are self-evident: they stand against "the system." However this does not extend as far as being anti-capitalist or standing for a system other than representative democracy. Rather, their opposition is to the "old-fashioned" coordinates of left and right. In their place is an anti-establishment stance "outside" the arrangements of coalitions and party pluralism; these latter are cast as corrupt. So we are presented with a binary moral conflict between an honest people endowed with "common sense," standing against the "cancer that is eating up our country and making the lives of honest people impossible."[4] At the same time the resistance to any ideological vision of politics leads both Podemos and M5S to approach government as a question of "problem-solving." Policies are treated alternately as technical solutions or as pragmatic ones rooted in common sense. The result is the same as the initial problem: an apolitical approach which we would recognize as "technocratic."

The challenge populism has put to technocracy throughout the End of History has resulted in a novel fusion: techno-populism. Channeling anti-establishment energy while maintaining an opposition to ideology and the left-right binary, the emerging techno-populist parties provide a synthesis that feels sadly appropriate to the End of the End of History – a strange creature wielding an angry, anti-political drive, but constrained by the deadening forms of the past. Variations on the theme can be found on the Right, too. The new Far-Right has tended to adopt a rhetoric of "neither left nor right" (Marine Le Pen's *Rassemblement National* in France; Geert Wilders' Freedom Party in the Netherlands), thereby repositioning these parties as *beyond* traditional political coordinates. Emmanuel Macron's centrist *La Republique en Marche*, the supposed upholder of the neoliberal order, is an amalgam of technocratic and populist elements.

Technical innovations have facilitated attempts to reinvigorate party politics. Availing themselves of social media and new digital platforms, technopopulists try to connect directly to rank-and-file members in a relationship departing strongly from older modes of party organizing. M5S's "Rousseau" platform allows members not only to vote in party primaries, but also to select which policies to adopt and even to participate in the drafting of laws. Other cases abound: Podemos has its Consul participation system, the Pirate Parties their LiquidFeedback democracy app, and *La France Insoumise* its NationBuilder software. All promise direct participation with the ostensible aim of reducing bureaucratic apparatuses and careerism on the part of cadres. This is a process called *disintermediation*: cutting out the middlemen in favor of a more immediate link between members and leader.[5]

Yet, as with commercial digital platforms, engagement is individualized, with little space for collective deliberation. So while members would no longer be passive and disengaged – as in the hollowed-out "television party" pioneered by Berlusconi, for instance – they are now not active but *reactive*. A member's engagement takes the form of a "narrow and ad-hoc response to the stimuli coming from above, sometimes supportive, sometimes critical, and in other cases still apathetic, to the prompting messages launched by the party leadership."[6]

This faux-democracy is evident in the plebiscitarianism on display: the leaders write the menu, members get served. The leader in this model is what Paolo Gerbaudo has called the *hyperleader*, the membership, the *superbase*. Because intermediary and representative party structures are absent, the party becomes dependent on the charismatic hyperleader to give it shape and direction.

This relationship extends beyond the question of digital platforms. Does the hyperleader not describe figures like Corbyn, Sanders, Iglesias or Mélenchon – not mere party leaders but in some way embodiments of all the members' hopes and dreams? The glorification of these figures has something of contemporary celebrity and fan culture to it. Witness the Bernie memes, or the cheering of Corbyn as the "Absolute Boy" – a semi-ironic nickname that seemed to invest in a reserved, undynamic politician a superhero status. These politicians do not project glamour as in traditional celebrity but rather are held as avatars of authenticity, honesty, moral courage, far beyond their mundane reality.

None of this is to dismiss or denigrate the return of political enthusiasm. It is important to believe in things – the cynicism of anti-politics is self-defeating. But the awkward, postmodern, semi-ironic idolatry foisted on the populist hyperleader is not conducive to democracy. The continuing weakness of the party form thus leaves the future uncertain.

Instead, the new populist party offers a limited politicization. There is a dual movement: the anti-political attack on the bureaucracy and hollowness of the neoliberal party says the masses matter. Simultaneously, it pulls the masses away again, fobbing them off with a restrictive, individualized form of participation. What has developed, then, is "a techno-populist party that combines new modes of participation and more established modes of self-appointed, expert-driven governance."[7] Moreover, we may even find emerging a more demagogic relationship, of leader-worship. It is almost as if, in trying to respond to the lack of popular trust in politics, we over-compensate and build idols out of compromised leaders such as Bernie Sanders in the US. In sum, the End of the End of History birthed left-populism, and that cycle has now come to an end. This moment also sees the final closing of social democracy, with traditional parties of the Center-Left continuing their death spiral. The one exception, the

UK Labour Party under Corbyn's leadership, has now rejoined the social-democratic pack. The past 5 years have proved to be merely a temporary lease-of-life. If "Pasokification" has become the accepted term for the evisceration of social-democratic parties[8], and "Syrizification" the boom and bust of left-populism, Labour is now suffering both, simultaneously. At least, though, over the past few years – and unlike in the 1990s and 2000s – it felt like we had something to lose.

In the next chapter we examine in more detail what is likely to follow left-populism and social democracy. But here we can conclude that a shift from anarchical resistance to party-based organized politics on the Left has been a key feature of recent years, representing an interrupted attempt at democratization. In the table below, these shifts, from the End of History to today, are laid out.

Table 7.1: The changing forms of the Left, 1989 to 2020

Period	Dominant	Mode of resistance	Political form	Examples	Social democracy
1989 – 2015	Post-politics	Neo-anarchist	Leaderless, "movement of movements," NGOs	Global justice movement, carnivalesque protest, humanitarian campaigns	Decline
2016 – 2020	Anti-politics	Left-populist	Left-populist parties, techno-populism	Podemos, Syriza, M5S, Corbyn, Sanders	Death

7.2 Protest all you like

The hollowing out of formal politics over the past decades – a process nearing nearly half a century in length – has led to repeated claims that, in fact, politics now happens elsewhere. As election turnouts began to decline from the late 1960s onwards, and party membership did even more starkly as of the same time, the New Social Movements around race, gender, sexuality and ecology picked up the slack. In the 1970s, social-democratic and corporatist arrangements felt the strain as formal politics overflowed with demands from outside. The argument that politics was happening "elsewhere" – beyond the realm of parliaments and parties – still had plausibility. But as formal participation fell into the abyss at the end of the Cold War, the notion that politics had simply been transplanted elsewhere became less and less convincing. In the 1990s and 2000s, the anti-globalization movement, consumer activism and various forms of protest were all breathlessly talked up as the new politics. All this ignored what had qualitatively changed: mass politics had evaporated.

Take the illustrative case of protests against the 2003 invasion of Iraq. In the anti-Iraq War demonstrations, extra-parliamentary forms of participation (some of the largest protests ever) proved fleeting, leading to little organization-building, wider radicalization or even political impact (Western wars in the Middle East would continue unabated). In the worst instances, activism was hopelessly narcissistic. Consumer activism – such as ethical consumerism – was only the most obvious example of a new form of "participation" that never went beyond individuated lifestyle politics. An aggregation of atomized, ethically informed choices never amounted to mass politics, no matter how many individuals took part (and mostly, the masses never did).

From the tweeness of Fairtrade campaigns to the militant anger of anti-corporate demos, "politics" in this period could largely be characterized as "ethical selving" – the creation of the self as an ethical, morally good subject. Inwardly directed, its social content amounted to the creation of radical subcultures, at best. Left-wing political activism became increasingly distant from the concerns, habits and outlooks of the broad working class.

If politics is inherently public, could this even be considered politics? It was more an aesthetic. As it was the middle and upper classes who always maintained a greater connection to formal politics, it was from their ranks that participants in informal politics at the End of History were drawn. The young, politicized middle-class person was able to don the garb of (radical) politics and play out a fantasy of "changing the world," completely removed from questions of state power.

Intersectionality, initially an attempt to regroup different but interlocking forms of oppression, has become perhaps the most prominent expression of public narcissism masquerading as politics. It shunned the question "what do *we* want to *achieve*?" in favor of asking "who am *I*?"; instead of "where are we going?" it recoiled from the future and pondered, "where did I come from?" This form of navel-gazing would eventually meet its evil twin in the form of the identity politics of the Right – yet both had shared the same umbilical cord.[9] As identity politics wound its way up from college campuses to the mainstream media, corporate marketing departments and international institutions, it came to appear a hegemonic force more than a radical challenge.

A new, "alternative" Right seized on the dislocations of the Global Financial Crisis lumping together "the Left" and neoliberalism. On the fringes, this New Right even revived an old (anti-Semitic) term, calling its antagonists "cultural Marxists." In doing so, it grouped together everyone from Davos "globalists" to left-wing anti-racists. As a consequence, today you have ranged against one another "progressive neoliberalism" on one side (everything from Davos Man to Black Lives Matters) and "reactionary populism" on the other.[10] These twin camps advance different forms of identity politics. Progressive neoliberals group together minority identities under the leadership of "globalists," while reactionary populists propose to speak for a majority "indigenous" identity in Western states supposedly threatened by migration.

One reason for this new stand-off is that new social movements are largely a product of a middle-class upsurge. To be clear, it is not that protests and social movements around the world in the 2010s were always composed of professionals and managers, nor that they only comprised the well-off. Often these protest movements embrace many precaritized workers and those economically struggling not least with urban property prices, whatever the nature of their labor. The point was rather that the politics of these movements was middle class in *character*. While working-class people may have participated in these protests, the protests themselves did not speak *as* or *for* the working class. The protests did not emerge from workplace struggles nor – with some notable exceptions – from working-class communities. Much less are they organized by self-consciously proletarian parties or movements. Bar some exceptions outside Europe and North America, nor were these revolts of the poor. Often, they are masses of angry individuals from all walks of life, coalescing momentarily in the streets – or online.

All of this is borne out by the data on labor militancy (see table 7.2, below). Nearly everywhere has seen steady or significant declines in labor militancy since the end of the Cold War. Even the uptick in general strikes in Europe during the Eurozone crisis of 2010-13 has quickly fallen back to near its long-term average. Neither the movement around Bernie Sanders nor the Corbyn-driven influx of new members into the British Labour Party were accompanied by a serious increase in labor militancy. Left politics may be back, but its usual driver is missing.

It could be argued that focusing on labor militancy is too restrictive a definition of "proper politics", and risks being oblivious to new forms of politicization. Yet it is worth highlighting the historical importance of working-class participation in forming modern democracy and mass politics. A recent study of one hundred years of protest demonstrates that

Table 7.2: Annual averages of work days lost due to industrial action per 1000 salaried employees, selected OECD countries[11]

	1985	1990	1995	2000	2005	2010	2015
Australia	223	207	79	61	26	13	8
Chile	x	78	96	29	23	64	55
France	727	528	784	581	164	318	74*
Germany	2	14	8	0	1	1	31
Italy	266	342	65	59	56	x	x
UK	304	84	19	21	9	15	6
US	73	55	51	161	13	2	5

democratizing reforms are much more readily achieved when the working class plays a major role in protest. By contrast, when protests are largely middle class, the evidence for social and political improvement is far more ambiguous.[12] This upsets liberal assumptions that protest from below is incipiently authoritarian and casts the educated, professional middle classes as the repository of liberal democratic norms. In sum: without significant working-class participation, protest fails.

Does the increasing frequency of protest not suggest that, because of the failures of establishment politics to represent people's desires, protest is the starting point for a new mass politics? Let us take a look at the composition of protests.

Systematic studies demonstrate that protests in Europe are younger and more middle class than the general population.[13] These are the same educated professionals that were classically identified as the main participants in the New Social Movements. Of course, there are differences according to the type of protest. Economic protests tend to be more working-class and instrumentally focused, whereas cultural protests tend to be more middle class and concerned with raising awareness. Nonetheless, broadly speaking, it is the young and middle class that are driving protest today. The divide is not only generational. There are two middle classes, divided socio-culturally. One is oriented toward the public sector comprising academics, public sector managers and professionals, lawyers, civil servants, teachers, etc., the other toward the market. It is the former group who are now increasingly mobilized in left-wing movements.

Before exploring this tension, it is worth noting some crucial exceptions. In France, the Gilets Jaunes (Yellow Vests) movement did not emerge as a labor struggle but as a consumer one. However, focused as it was on the cost of living, it was naturally more plebeian than the anarchic anti-globalization protests of the 1990s and early 2000s. This was visible in its composition too, which not only came "from below" but also "from outside": activists were mainly drawn from a hinterland of mid-size and small towns and rural areas, where the movement was birthed. French inequality increasingly has a geographic character, with the urban metropolises sucking up wealth, resources and talent while the provinces are left to stagnate. Rent and other costs in cities like Paris skyrocket and urban cores become increasingly unaffordable. They consequently become home to either well-off professionals and the precarious service class that ministers to their needs. The Left in recent times has tended to appeal mainly to the radicalized middle classes, or to sections of the immigrant working class in big cities, often on identitarian rather than economic grounds. At the same time, the Left lost connection to the broad working class in industrial and especially post-industrial smaller cities. Yet it was from these latter "left behind" areas that the Yellow Vests exploded onto the national scene in France.

The example is raised here because, if the return of politics is to become a truly mass phenomenon, the Yellow Vests seem a more plausible vision than protests like the Climate Strike – to take one example – which is dominated by the middle classes. If labor union density is at historic lows, and grandiose calls for a general strike evince weakness more than strength, then social movements based around distribution and consumption – rather than production – appear more promising.

If nothing else, the shunning of the Yellow Vests by the media and the liberal-left intelligentsia in France (be it for their immoderation, or for breaking with environmentalist orthodoxy around higher fuel costs, or for being "racist" – the go-to slur nowadays whenever the working class starts to move) should indicate the potential of that movement. That this protest turned on the same kind of geographical inequalities that have become so readily apparent in nearly every rich country in the global North suggests a certain replicability.

7.3 The radicalized middle

The emergence of a new Left, ranged around Corbyn's election as leader of the Labour Party in the UK and Bernie Sanders' campaign to become the Democratic contender for the US presidency, suggests radicalization. However, since these developments were not borne by labor mobilization, what drove it? One explanation frequently tendered is that downwardly mobile members of the middle class, especially Millennials and Zoomers (i.e. the two generations born since 1981), have turned leftwards. Politicized by the closing of employment opportunities and the burden of rising student debt and urban housing costs, the figure of the "graduate without a future" propelled the new politics. The flagship policies adopted by the Bernie Sanders and Jeremy Corbyn campaigns around free higher education are suggestive of this shift.

The role of education is certainly one of the principal pivots of contemporary politics. Higher education has expanded significantly in the US and UK over preceding decades. Those with completed tertiary education increased from 20.7 percent to 26.8 percent in the US from 1990 to 2010. The enrollment rate for 18-24 year-olds similarly increased from 32 percent to 40.5 percent between 1990 and 2015. In the UK, those with completed tertiary education increased from 9 percent to 15.3 percent between 1990-2010, and the participation rate (those in higher education up to the age of 30) reached 50.2 percent in the latest year for which figures are available (2017/18).[14]

As information technology and other changes to labor processes destroyed less-skilled white-collar jobs, so political elites pushed higher education as a means of preparing a workforce for the new economy. This of course was a lie, as there were not enough new, well-paying jobs to mop up those new degree-bearing graduates – especially not after the GFC. A generation faced the prospect of being worse off than their parents, and history tends to show that nothing radicalizes like dashed expectations. But this encounter with left-wing politics on the part of sections of the middle class was naturally different from that of blue-collar workers or marginalized groups in previous eras. Would these young middle-class people be a significant enough base to build a new radical politics around? And would they be good allies to the traditional working class? Clarity can be found by examining a debate that has recently emerged around the meaning and political proclivities of the "professional-managerial class" (PMC).

PMC has increasingly been wielded as an epithet to criticize better-off progressives whose involvement in left-wing politics has brought with it forms of divisive identity politics and sundry narcissistic pathologies. Yet the "Professional-Managerial Class" was originally devised as a sociological concept by Barbara and John Ehrenreich in the 1970s.[15] The Ehrenchreichs analyzed how the New Left of the 1960s and 70s related to the working class in distinct ways, seeming to be a part of it but at the same time separate. What they termed the professional-managerial class was neither the big bourgeoisie (owners of capital) nor the old middle class of self-employed professionals such as doctors and lawyers, or small tradespeople, independent farmers and so on. Often they were employed in large corporations and organizations, like the working class, but occupied roles as managers, academics, teachers, administrators, technical workers, cultural producers, doctors, lawyers, etc., so they were functionally distinct from blue-collar workers. As the Ehrenreichs put it, these were "salaried mental workers who do not own the means of production and whose major function in the social division of labor may be described broadly as the reproduction of capitalist culture and capitalist class relations."[16]

The PMC, therefore, is not a class, properly speaking. It does not have a structurally antagonistic relationship to either capital or labor, nor is it a residuum like the petty bourgeoisie (small owners, many of whom were wiped out in earlier phases of capitalist development); it is a product of monopoly capitalism. This ambiguous position allows members of the PMC to go either way, to take either side in the class struggle, depending on context.

In advanced capitalist societies, the growth of service-sector jobs relying on "immaterial labor" in the "knowledge economy" has driven greater swathes of the population to pursue higher education, swelling the ranks of the PMC. But then the GFC came along and split this rising stratum. In a 2013 reflection on the matter, Barbara Ehrenreich noted that the class now lies in ruins:

> At its wealthier end, skilled professionals continue to jump ship for more lucrative posts in direct service to capital: scientists give up their research to become "quants" on Wall Street; physicians can double their incomes by finding work as investment analysts for the finance industry or by setting up "concierge" practices serving the wealthy. At the less fortunate end of the spectrum, journalists and PhDs in sociology or literature spiral down into the retail workforce.

In between, health workers and lawyers and professors find their work lives more and more hemmed in and regulated by corporation-like enterprises.[17]

This downward mobility is nothing that different to what the old industrial working class faced decades earlier through deindustrialization. Old secure jobs are wiped out and acquired skills become redundant or, at any rate, no longer find valorization in the market. The old PMC analyzed by the Ehrenreichs was motivated by a spirit of professionalism, and envisaged a society ruled by reason, in which they assumed intellectual, if not political, leadership. This arrangement has now been discredited.

The upshot is that, on the one hand, the upper sections of the PMC, especially those who make up or are aligned with the political class, have suffered Neoliberal Order Breakdown Syndrome. The economic currents and political relations that promoted them to an enviable position in society have proved to be unsustainable, and now the barbarians are at the gates. The society they thought to be ruled by reason is now under challenge. Hence the panic about "fake news" and "post-truth" – a charge of unreason hurled at those who would seek to disrupt their comfortable arrangements and especially their social and political authority. On the other hand, the downwardly mobile sections of the PMC – and especially younger generations who have been impacted more acutely by rising rents and tuition fees than older generations who pursued higher education and bought property at less burdensome costs – have been driven to left-wing politics. This has energized social demands around material questions, especially concerning health, housing and education, across North America and Western Europe, targeting decades of neoliberal austerity.

The downside has been to entrain some questionable politics in tow. Amber A'Lee Frost has depicted these issues as they afflict the Democratic Socialists of America (DSA), the organization to have most benefited from the transformations just described. "Unlike a functioning union, DSA, for all its alleged antagonism to capitalism, isn't particularly antagonistic to capitalists. It does however produce innumerable segregated 'working groups,' hyphenated interest clusters, extensive grievance policies, and long lists of priority-less political demands, all of which appeal to the anxieties of the PMC, many of whom have fallen – and can't get up."[18] This is a product of the tendency on the part of members of the PMC to not acknowledge their class interests, precisely because their formation emphasizes disinterested expertise. This generates pathologies whereby the PMC projects their concerns onto the working class, assuming themselves as the latter's guardian. When this finds few takers, the reaction can turn nasty.

7.4 Fighting the wrong war

Unfortunately, the upsurge in left-wing activism has gone hand-in-hand with "the great awokening," as journalist Matthew Yglesias termed it. In the US, white liberals have radicalized significantly over the past decade on race, gender and sexuality.[19] "Intersectionality" is largely a means for highly educated liberals to gain distinction, and for the upper stratum of minority groups to leverage themselves into positions of influence. Worse, it recasts material relations as symbolic ones, such that, for example, a black woman's problems could only be a consequence of racial and gender oppression, and unique to her existence as a black woman. Solidarity across racial/gender/sexuality lines is then impossible or unnecessary. She is only appealed to as a black woman, and never as a worker or citizen. The radicalization of cultural liberalism has become so pronounced that a member of the Combahee River Collective, the New Left group of black lesbian feminists that coined the term "identity politics," even took a stand against the fragmentation and self-centeredness prompted by its contemporary manifestations, and endorsed Bernie Sanders[20] – a politician slandered by PMC liberals for supposedly not paying due attention to race and gender.[21]

A related development – one which also stands oblique, if not outright contrary, to class politics – is a new, angry generational politics. Captured in the "OK, Boomer" meme, it charges those who came of age in earlier decades to have unduly burdened subsequent generations. Benefiting from cheaper housing and free college, Baby-Boomers are held to be responsible for generational inequality and – in its most confrontational formulation – to have despoiled the planet, leaving nothing to younger generations.

As real as generational inequalities are, it does not follow that *generational politics* present any resolution. The fact that older generations may be relatively better off does not mean they are the "winners" of social development. Polarization along generational lines like this only serves to obscure class as the fundamental relation shaping society. Indeed, generational warfare is a specifically middle-class pathology today. It is the child criticizing their parents for not giving them their "due." The entitlement is obvious. Provoked by downward mobility, the inability to reproduce itself as a class, or to reproduce at an individual level the standard of living their parents had, the youth wing of the PMC turns to generational politics to explain its difficulties.

The developments sketched here are suggestive of significant political realignments in process. Of course, not every middle-class person has suddenly become left-wing, nor, for that matter, has the working class become right-wing *en masse* – that would be to adopt the propaganda of right-wing populists. But understanding how the middle class is changing shines a light on the politics of our age.

Joel Kotkin, an American geographer, notes the relative decline of the traditional middle class of small business owners, minor landowners, craftspeople and artisans. In tandem, we see the ascendancy of the (upper reaches of the) PMC. For Kotkin, this class fragment is the "new clerisy."[22] In opting for this term – taken from Samuel Coleridge, who used it in the 1830s to describe religious orders – Kotkin draws our attention to the *ideological* role it plays. Found in public and quasi-public institutions such as universities, the media, NGOs and the state bureaucracy, its main function is not economic production but production of culture and morals. The new clerisy is generally favorable to the state, accepting of higher taxes and regulation. According to Michael Lind, this stratum accounts for maybe 15 percent of society today in the US.[23] For Kotkin, it has no structural antagonism with the oligarchy, because it is the latter who fund their NGOs, universities and so on.

In France, Christophe Guilluy has observed similar tendencies. For him, the metropolitan, educated, upper-middle class has convinced itself class does not exist. In the past, its traditional equivalents were keenly aware of class struggle, so consequently were more elitist and defended order, tradition and morality. Today this new class prizes, above all, openness, modernity and diversity. But diversity is something they demand for others while they reside in gentrified urban cores, thus not accepting genuine diversity where they live. This relatively privileged stratum operates from an assumption of moral superiority, all the while not acknowledging the existence of hierarchy.[24]

It is noteworthy that anti-political revolts have primarily targeted this section of the middle class, to its dismay. As Amber A'Lee Frost has remarked, when this stratum "hears the phrase 'liberal elite' to refer to the progressive PMC, they assume it can be nothing more than a dog whistle, meant to incite working-class resentment against themselves."[25] Instead, they ask, why not attack the business elite, for they are responsible for your problems? But the ire directed against educated liberals is real. The business class, and the Center-Right parties to which it is aligned, may hold and defend economic power, but it is relatively amoral. It preaches self-interest and the market. If you don't trust politics, then looking after yourself and yours seems like the safest option. The Center-Right may hawk a miserly vision but it promises no more than that. The Center-Left abrogates for itself a moral mission, to make society more progressive. Its intimate identification with the sphere of politics, then, suggests that its only goal is to lord it over everyone else.

Should this description appear unfounded, consider French economist Thomas Piketty's recent work. In a multidimensional analysis of inequality, Piketty concludes that the Left has become the party of the intellectual elite (what he terms the Brahmin Left), while the Right can be viewed as the party of the business elite (or the Merchant Right). Based on post-election surveys conducted in the US, UK and France, from the postwar period until today, Piketty's research demonstrates how left-wing parties have gone from being workers' parties to parties of the highly educated.[26] The Left[27] today has a higher share of the vote among university graduates than non-university graduates, and the educational top 10 percent's participation in the left-wing vote outweighs the educational bottom 90 percent. Consequently, "left vs right" does not map onto class lines. Instead, the Left represents high-education voters and the Right, lower-education voters. This has created a 'multi-elite' party system, in which the intellectual and business elites face off, each cobbling together coalitions from the rest of society.

Perhaps even more striking is that a reversal is under way on income lines too, such that the left-wing vote is becoming both high-income and high-education, while the Right attracts low-income and low-education voters, representing an almost total realignment of the party system. Of course, the parties categorized as "left" are not particularly left-wing, but as the Radical Left's share of the vote is small or almost non-existent, what we have is an electoral face-off between liberal and conservative parties, with the former increasingly being the party of the well-heeled and well-educated.

As a consequence of this realignment, politics now often plays out in globalist-vs-nativist terms. As turnout rates decline at the lower ends of the income and education scales, this is an electoral polarization that mainly plays out within the middle class, broadly conceived. So just as the young, downwardly mobile PMC has radicalized leftwards, so the old, market-oriented petty bourgeoisie has turned harshly against liberalism, voting for Trump, UKIP/Brexit Party, or Le Pen's *Rassemblement National*.[28]

What we find, then, is primarily a *culture* war. The breakdown of the neoliberal order has opened up the possibility of politics. The dislocations may lead up the path to class polarization, to consciousness of a society divided between laborers who produce and capitalists who reap the rewards; but our age also opens other paths. Cultural polarization – culture war – is a downward spiral that has opened up in front of us. And, as it is fully capable of capturing and organizing popular anger, it presents a genuine danger. As the historian of US culture wars Andrew Hartman has noted, "cultural conflict has fused with class-based discord to create an unusually toxic politics."[29] The old culture wars which polarized the US from the 1960s were fought over sexuality, religion and the family. Today, they are more closely linked to changing economic circumstances, with globalization, immigration and identity the key dividing lines. And the internet has exacerbated these tensions, with the cultural left provoking a vicious reaction by a postmodern Right – as cataloged by Angela Nagle's study of the "alt-right."[30]

In the US, there is scant evidence of a polarization among the broad mass of the population. What has occurred is party sorting, such that the Democrats and Republicans have become more ideologically homogenous, moving away from the more diffuse and broadly-based "catch-all" parties that they were in the past. But more than just homogeneity in political positions, homogeneity in geographic, behavioral, attitudinal, religious and educational characteristics has obtained as well. The secular, coastal, socially liberal woman with a graduate degree is therefore increasingly likely to be a Democrat; this is not mere stereotype. The political polarization that Donald Trump and Bernie Sanders' support testifies to, then, is a product of radicalization among the already-politicized.[31] This, too, is another facet of a middle class that has split into rival camps who spar along class-inflected but ultimately cultural lines.

It is not just the US that is riven by new culture wars: the UK and even continental European countries have fallen to similar divisions. Consider France's anti-gay marriage movement or, most strikingly, the protests in solidarity with the death of George Floyd that emerged from the UK to Denmark to New Zealand. Wokeness has gone global. Indeed, class-inflected culture wars have broken out far from the developed West. In 2015, South Africa was riven by the Rhodes Must Fall protests. Brazil, over the period described in more depth in Chapter 5, has polarized between *antipetista* and progressive camps[32], with the former eventually electing Jair Bolsonaro in 2018. Although they may use the language of class, the protagonists in this struggle do not break along class lines – it is a culture war between middle-class camps, each purporting to represent the masses, albeit in different ways. Turkey's culture wars have been widely discussed, but they, too, appear to interlink with class in ambiguous ways. The 2013 protests in Gezi park were in principle a rejection of neoliberalism, but they were dominated by the better-educated middle class, whereas Erdogan's base has been the provincial petty bourgeoisie.

Unfortunately, until the working class and labor starts to move and speak with its own voice, we are left with this conundrum: what do we do about the left-leaning PMC, given its ability to alternately support and sabotage socialist politics?

The standard response is that center-left parties' adoption of culturally progressive values at the expense of economically redistributive policies is what has lost them working-class support (undoubtedly true); so, therefore, re-incorporating material demands will resolve the problem. And yet, the adoption of economically redistributive policies has not won back the workers, to which Corbyn's failure testifies.

Returning to where we began this chapter, the "void" still confronts us, and it will not be bridged by policy promises alone. The actual atrophy of intermediating organizations (unions, local party branches, social clubs) and the vast cultural distance between working-class citizens and left-wing activists mean simply pivoting "leftwards" does not suffice. When there is so little trust in politics, promises are just words on a page. When they come from the ranks of the progressive PMC and via the same parties that previously abandoned the working class, it would take a huge leap of faith to vest one's future in them.

Disentangling the cross-stitch of demographic divisions that have strained with the breakdown of the neoliberal order is therefore essential, so that genuine class antagonism can be seen clearly. The fact that expressions of class antagonism may not conform to the expectations of politesse cultivated in online debates by PMC liberals will undoubtedly scare off many on the Left. This was visible in the reaction to the Yellow Vests or to Brexit. Neither are unambiguous expressions of working-class revolt, but it is the nature of the End of the End of History that means that class politics will emerge in different forms. The task for the Left is to extract the radical kernel from the shell.

Chapter 8

Ideologies of the Near Future

The defining political characteristic of our age is the loss of authority of political establishments and the simultaneous weakness of a Left unable to seize the moment. If anti-politics is the predominant political force today, then how establishment forces respond to it will give shape to society. Already the figure of techno-populism, explored in the previous chapter, suggests a coming synthesis of forces previously thought antagonistic: populism and technocracy. The success or otherwise of establishment responses to the Covid-19 crisis, and to the crumbling of neoliberalism, will determine the lines of political antagonism over the next decade.

As we saw in Chapter 3, it is the Left that brings politics into being, by politicizing "business-as-usual." Therefore, consciousness of the Left's weakness is essential to understanding our era. We should briefly rehearse the key features here. The organized working class was defeated across the Western world and beyond across the 1980s and early 1990s. This was the essential constitutive element of the "End of History" thesis: the absence of an organized working-class challenge to liberal capitalism. Then, through a series of long-term processes of elite withdrawal from the rest of society, and citizens' concomitant withdrawal into the private sphere, contemporary politics came to be defined by a *void* between the citizenry and politics. The means for representing popular interests at the level of the state are now greatly reduced. Though the Cold War arrangements were no golden age, the contrast to our times is stark: democratic participation has withered, state power has become correspondingly more high-handed and remote.

Through the End of History period, social-democratic

parties in Europe stopped being even the electorally significant managers of neoliberalism to become instead utterly marginal – they were *Pasokified*.[1] More recently, the left-populism that offered itself as a potential reboot for left politics in Europe broke itself on the rock of the EU, leading to a wave of defeat, from the capsizing of Syriza to the death of Corbynism.[2] We are now seeing a whole set of political realignments that throw into question moribund alliances, such as between the working class and the Labour Party in the UK.[3] It was in this context that the novel coronavirus was the *coup de grace* to left-populism, with center-right forces outflanking their political opponents in the aftermath of the pandemic.

If the Left has often been a coalition between progressive liberals and socialists, then we can generalize across a number of different contexts and conclude that the Left today is dominated by its liberal wing. Traditionally, the Left understood the working class in two related but distinct ways. The working class was seen as the *object* of politics, with the welfare of the working-class majority to be improved through redistribution, large social projects and economic development. At the same time, the working class was also seen as the *subject* of politics, with the goal of working-class self-government held as the defining aim of politics and class struggle. In broad terms we can say the latter represents a socialist approach to the working class, foregrounding agency, while liberals and reformers of all stripes are more comfortable with the former, putting the emphasis on welfare. While often combined in struggles for democracy and improved conditions of work, the significance of liberal domination of the Left today is that there are now very few defenders of the notion of the working class as the *subject* of politics. What has filled that space is a range of cultural arguments – around community, belonging and the nation – most often led by the Right.

The Covid-19 crisis put into doubt a whole range of other

issues. To cite just a few: the resilience and desirability of globally integrated supply chains; the profitability and continued existence of small and medium-sized businesses; independent central banks' role in tightly controlling the money supply – and indeed, their very independence; working arrangements and commuting; or relatively loose border controls. And that was before the longer-term economic and political consequences fully manifested themselves. Of course, the expectation that economic recession and dislocations will radicalize people is misguided. The Covid-19 crisis was an exogenous shock, which turned attention onto how politicians dealt with the crisis, rather than the operations of capitalism itself. But even if Covid-19 were to be followed by an endogenous crisis – say, originating in China's debt pile-up – this would not necessarily prove propitious to the Left. The point is rather that the "great moderation" of the 90s and 00s is now long gone – the future will be turbulent, and that at least promises to throw up new possibilities.

Neoliberalism is decisively breaking down, and has been already discredited in many parts of the world. This, though, has more been a product of its internal contradictions than due to external challenge. The political authority of neoliberalism has waned as it has proved unable to provide increased standards of living for the majority, nor any meaningful sense of social purpose. At present, a range of options seem possible for a post-neoliberal settlement. The argument of this chapter is in large part an attempt to map this existing disorganization of politics and to propose three new poles which may emerge in future.

8.1 Responses to the breakdown of the neoliberal order

The pandemic has revealed a double weakness: the weakness of states across the globe in managing coronavirus and protecting their citizens, but also the weakness of the left response to the pandemic and the very real challenges of creating a compelling alternative to the one offered by capitalism.[4] Drawing out trends that preceded – and in many cases have been accelerated by – the Covid-19 crisis, we predict that the politics of the coming decade will appear strange to observers who assume that the old Left/ Right template of the late Cold War era will return, after the End of the End of History. In fact, those organizations and sections of society that claim the legacy of the Center-Left may end up defending the status quo ante, while a new Right proposes reformist or reactionary challenges to liberal capitalism.

Synthesizing phenomena from a range of national contexts – though focused on Europe and North America – we can outline three different responses. The broad, post-neoliberal center ground will edge its way to a more state-capitalist model, promoting greater public expenditure and investment, as well as an attention to the regional inequalities that have developed across advanced industrial societies in the past 30 years. This post-neoliberal conservatism will make a plausible push to be the hegemonic ideology of the next decade and to provide the basis of a post-coronavirus settlement. In order to do so, it will need to co-opt sections of the masses, be it downwardly mobile middle classes, the old working class or new, precaritized workers – or most likely, some combination of these. In the most basic terms: it will move "left" economically and "right" on cultural issues.

What is called "liberalism" in North America – in Europe, the liberal-left or the institutional Left – is likely to see politics as a process of managing conflict and will draw its impetus for change from a fundamentally charitable, moral impulse. Left-liberalism in the coming decade is therefore best understood as "progressive technocracy." As the technocratic mode of government is separated from its neoliberal shell, so the Center-Left will embrace it even more wholeheartedly, now that it is unburdened by its association with neoclassical economics. This should come as no surprise, as this "Left" will represent the interests, above all, of the professional-managerial class, characterized by their high cultural capital and fealty to disinterested rationality. It will be an irony of history that in the coming decade those identifying with the "Left" will do the most to defend and extend (the "progressive" aspects of) neoliberalism – evidence-based policy, multicultural "tolerance", globalization, etc.

If the new Center-Right becomes more nationalist, both in its economic policy and in its discourse, then what of the reactionary Far-Right? The success of the new establishment in incorporating anti-political energies will determine the strength of reactionary forces. If a more reformist Center-Right represents an attempt to relegitimate capitalism, at the expense of some concessions from the high bourgeoisie, then reactionary ideologies may speak for a resentful petty bourgeoisie (especially if state responses to the Covid-19 crisis are unable to provide for the long-term prospects of small business owners). Although it is difficult to predict the exact forms that reaction will take, two strands are likely to increase in prominence: a form of authoritarian populism, based on longing for a strong leader and strong state to compensate for the lack of political authority; and a Malthusian narrative emphasizing limited resources, with a concomitant need to reduce surplus populations, removing outsiders and other elements seen as corrupting the "indigenous" population.

As should be clear from this presentation, the mainstream Right will innovate, while the Left will stagnate. This is fundamentally due to left-liberal abhorrence of the nation and the masses that compose it. Unable to respond either to conservative desires for belonging, nor radical ones for sovereign democracy, the liberal Left will seek escape in various other terrains, looking back nostalgically to the age of globalization.

Table 8.1: The structure of ideological conflict, 2020s

Characteristic ideology	Location on spectrum	Key ideas	Tone/ Discourse	Corresponding class interests
State-Capitalism / Post-Neoliberal Conservatism / Corporatism	Center to Right	State-led investment Address regional disparities Renegotiate globalization Ethical/social constraints to capitalist enterprise Incorporation of sections of masses	Soft Nationalist / Communitarian / Populist	Middle class, sections of working class; Concessions from capitalist class
Progressive Technocracy	Center-Left	Technological saviorism, green supranationalism Intersectionality Anti-fascism/"popular front" Moral minoritarianism	Moralistic / Technocratic / Alternately alarmist and superficially optimistic	Professional-managerial class; Woke sections of capital
Authoritarian Populism	Far-Right	Anti-immigrant populism Organicism (ecological conception of nation) Strengthen repressive state apparatus Response to "crisis of authority" through empowering individual leader	Anti-Political / Xenophobic	Petty bourgeoisie, sections of old working class

8.2 State-capitalism: the new Center-Right

There will be – already is – a conservative and nationalist turn from the traditional forces of order. Having adopted neoliberalism up to two generations ago, the Covid-19 crisis will drive these forces to innovate in an attempt to win voters: having lost its professional class backers, it will attempt to capture downwardly mobile middle-class, as well as working-class, voters. The functional upshot of this would be to reconstruct legitimacy for capitalism through key reforms. We may see the development of a model of post-neoliberal conservatism, which looks to ally the traditional class interests of capital with parts of the working-class "left behind," and left cold, by progressive neoliberalism. Though some austere neoliberal policies will no doubt remain, establishments will edge toward a model of state-capitalism, promoting greater public expenditure and investment. Continuing "lowflation" means room for maneuver in the leading states will be significant, at least where they are monetarily sovereign. State borrowing and money-printing will continue in a drive for growth, and in order to incorporate sections of the masses in this new national project.

As post-neoliberal conservatives attempt to establish hegemonic projects, it is likely that visions of "ethical capitalism," which in a previous era focused on individual consumers, will be applied to corporate structures and national policies. For instance, in August 2019, the Business Roundtable group of CEOs of the largest American firms dropped from their definition of the purpose of a corporation Milton Friedman's famous "shareholder first" dictum. Instead, they asserted that corporations should aim to "improve society," while also treating employees, the environment, and their business practices ethically.[5] The business class's felt lack of legitimacy and popular support, and their fears of insurrection, will see them extend "ethical" approaches to more traditional, material concerns.[6] As *Financial Times* editor Lionel Barber put it in their "New Agenda" brand platform launch in September 2019: "The long-term health of free enterprise capitalism will depend on delivering profit with purpose."[7] One means of underscoring this may be through flaunting their reshoring efforts and domestic job-creation, rather than doing so on liberal gender and race grounds.

One model of the new, more nationalist center-right politics is found in Boris Johnson's Conservative Party in the UK. To a large extent, Brexit – and then the Covid-19 crisis – broke a path for post-neoliberal conservatism in creating the political necessity for large-scale state intervention, illustrating how quickly austerity positions were abandoned. In Johnson's approach, we may witness a combination of big government and anti-liberal values, representing a renewal of an old model of "One-Nation Conservatism." As one of the authors of the Tories' 2019 manifesto put it, it is an appeal to people with conservative values ("they want criminals to be punished") but who are also heavily reliant on the state and its services.[8] This post-neoliberal conservatism is pitched as a middle route, between the negative consequences of hyper-globalization on the one side and a hard-right nationalist populism on the other. A means of doing so will be to lessen the divergence between metropolitan centers and mid-size towns and rural areas. This would win the Center-Right new constituencies in which it perhaps never found support, such as from the old working class in rust-belt areas. The question for the medium-term viability of this project is the extent to which those sections of the working class that have been attracted to this project can be retained; one of the key factors will, of course, be whether the Left is successful in attempts to win back these heartlands, or if it instead turns away from them as irredeemably lost, racist, xenophobic and so on.[9]

The Johnson government is but one model, led by the traditional elite, attempting to soften the "hard but hollow" state. The Republican Party in the US has already repulsed most professional elites, and is now an uneasy alliance between its donor class (who are only there "because they are not smart enough to recognize that the Democratic Party offers a far more effective reputation laundering service")[10] and a voter base that hates these donors. The party is thus a more demotic affair than the Democrats; should an arrangement with its donor base be found (say, offering protectionism to certain sectors), its transformation into strategist Steve Bannon's dreamed-of "working-class party" would continue.[11] Trump already began this process, mobilizing anti-political sentiment. The political and class realignment underway would strengthen this dynamic. It may well have a more nativist thrust, seeking to buy-off – and indeed create – loyal subjects on racialized bases, in a new corporatism with shades of authoritarian populism (the third ideological pole, to be discussed below).

In Germany, the CDU-CSU is already facing internal pressures to move rightward. While relenting on the punishing austerity inflicted on the European periphery may not be on the cards, a more statist and nationalist arrangement *at home* may well be. In France, Macron's abandonment of neoliberal reforms may point the way to a faux-Gaullism, with more *dirigiste* economic policies and protectionism outflanking the perpetual challenge of Len Pen's post-fascist grouping. Abandoning – or dragging-along – his professional class supporters may prove of little cost in contrast to the potential gains.

8.3 Progressive technocracy: the new Center-Left

The institutional Left will find itself in an even more challenging position than it does now. There are a number of reasons why the Left could easily fall into the historically paradoxical position of bolstering a crumbling neoliberal order. Already, what most characterizes the Center-Left voter is their higher educational attainment. This suggests a major realignment is underway, as the class alliance between the state-oriented middle class and the organized working class withers. Nominally "Left" parties and movements are likely to continue to be strongly influenced by the interests, concerns and values of the professional-managerial class. There are, of course, other relevant demographic cleavages: the Left is younger, more female, more urban, and more socially and culturally liberal, but none of these characteristics will give it the social majority necessary to create a hegemonic bloc, or even to reliably win elections, if it is unable to persuade working-class voters it can offer them real material gains. The evidence so far is that the Left's PMC composition has the effect of building-in sympathy for existing institutions, preventing it from seeking political rupture – necessary to make radical alternatives more than just words on a page.

Second, this Left would not have an independent ideological orientation. Social-democratic parties have been discredited by their accommodation with neoliberalism across the globe. Left-populism promised a reinvigoration of these parties, or the creation of new parties that would displace old ones on this end of the spectrum. Although we have argued throughout that this moment has passed, the effect of shifting values among the Center-Left's voters may be to push existing parties "to the left" on certain issues – on intersectionalist grounds, on the environment or on certain aspects relating to public services. But what we mean by lack of "independence" is that this positioning will be parasitic on the moves made by the new, nationalist center ground. The Center-Left will find itself to be offering nothing more than moral and technical criticisms of ruling parties, rather than being rooted in a viewpoint which is materially antagonistic to them.

The Left will propose a combination of managerial and humanitarian politics that we call progressive technocracy. It is the promotion of a "progressive" agenda without challenging the interests of capital – indeed, this could even be seen as representing the far-left flank of capital. Although progressive technocracy is already the official ideology of institutional center-left parties (such as the Democrats), this ideology will extend much further, into the "socialist" Left. Indeed, there will likely be a fusion between these camps.

Already, we have seen the battle lines drawn over the sanitary responses to the pandemic. The Left rallied to technocracy: it insisted narrowly on "following the science", and on lockdowns. Dissenting voices mainly came from the Right. The left-wing response to governments has been to insist on better and smarter implementation of policy, or to criticize policies for their unequal consequences (e.g. for negative consequences falling harder on ethnic minorities). This is not an opposition of principle, but a moral and technical fine-tuning. The Center-Right sets the tune, the Center-Left marches along, correcting for pitch and tempo. What we are seeing here is in fact a dress rehearsal for the coming battle over climate change politics.

Green New Deal-like programs are likely to become mainstream in the aftermath of Covid-19, and may well be implemented by governments of the Center and Right. Of course, they will probably prove inadequate in significantly reducing emissions and pursuing a clean energy transition, but as their electoral base is more involved in direct production (either as workers or owners of productive capital), they will be sensitive to negative impacts on living standards. The Center-Left, rooted in the public sector, the "non-governmental sector" and "immaterial" production, will have no such qualms and will be free to push for more aggressive emissions targets, oblivious to material concerns. The consequences for its public support will be negative, as is visible in the Gilets Jaunes challenge to Macron. Any success the Center-Left has in influencing policy direction will be through politicians adopting technical proposals, or in pursuing the more punitive inflections of environmentalism.

The radical elements found in contemporary "socialist" proposals for a GND – such as a guaranteed jobs program or the socialization of investment – will not find takers. Put off by the liberal, anti-popular aspects of environmental politics, the working class will not align behind the radical GND proposals. To see this sort of program put into action would require the Left to root its demands in the material interests of the masses (for example: for increased mobility, for more living space, even if that means suburbanization; and so on). The Left's aversion to the nation, to large numbers of its own citizens, will prevent it from taking up these sorts of demands; the socialist Left will remain hitched to its liberal wing, to its downfall.

The mantra, instead, will be that global problems require global solutions. Having failed to win executive power at the national level, it will seek to act at the supranational dimension, as a way of evading the need to win majority support nationally. The appeal is that supposed gains or preferred solutions could be "locked-in" (i.e., insulated from democratic input) – especially for environmental policies.[12] Repeated failure to make serious advances at this level, and the fact other forces will be returning to the national level as the key scale of governance, will not stop the liberal-left. The launch in 2020 of the global Progressive International builds on the failed attempts of DiEM-25 to gain traction at a European level, and already points the way in this direction. As an attempt to counter Bannon's "Nationalist International," it will founder: the working class has failed for decades to seize the national state, why would it now be capable of acting at an even higher level? The short-cut of circumventing national politics will not succeed. Indeed, it is fated to fail: it will instead form part of a wider retreat from the terrain of the nation-state and national democracy. The anti-majoritarian drift may even see the Left turn to the judiciary as a "neutral" arbiter of political conflicts, finding it has no sway over (increasingly hollowed-out) representative bodies.

The retreat from the nation will not only be "up" and "sideways," but downwards too. The Center-Left will propose a range of measures designed to promote "civic engagement" or "community participation." Citizens' Assemblies have already been convened to offer the UK government climate advice.[13] Citizens' summits, juries and panels all aim at participation rather than power, at the technocratic incorporation of the people into politics in order to manage away conflict. Likewise the popularity of deliberative modes of engagement, deliberative stakeholder events or workshops are characteristic tools of technocratic do-gooders as they create the simulacrum of a democratic process in which people are assembled to provide an ostensibly collective solution to a problem, but decisions lack a binding quality or have already been taken in advance. Though unable to gain traction at a transnational level, the Left may find some success in municipal politics, following the 2010s example of Barcelona.[14] This will be a means of hunkering down in urban centers – the so-called "rebel cities" – that are the Left's stronghold.

The "technological" aspect of technocracy may also be accentuated by the Center-Left, as can be illustrated in visions of "Fully Automated Luxury Communism" (FALC) or in the contemporary incarnation of the Californian Ideology.[15] If this Left's predominant tone will be doomy and moralistic, these elements will provide an optimistic counterpoint. In FALC we see the construction, through an extrapolation of today's technological trends, of a potential age of abundance in which living standards are considerably higher than the present. However, it is also a depoliticized vision, in which political change is achieved not through mass participation but by technological fiat. It is a world beyond work and capitalism, but one achieved by genetic editing and renewable energies rather than through collective political struggle. The masses are not required to enact political change, and are instead bought off with material improvements; in turn, these material improvements come to *compensate* for the lack of individual and collective control over conditions of life or work. Although FALC is unlikely to come to pass, various post-work ideas may flourish, such as a Universal Basic Income or reducing working time. These may well be adopted by governments but, without working-class power, they will be means of appeasing workers, masking unemployment and/or cutting public services. In this vision, nothing is too good for the working class – except self-determination.

Similarly, we can see in the ideology of Silicon Valley a mix of hippie and yuppie ideas combined with a faith in the liberatory promise of technology. Its left-wing inflection will see an attempt to solve social problems through technical means, making use of left-wing support among tech workers. But, as Evgeny Morozov has explained, there is a crushing circularity to this logic: only those issues that can be solved by tech are defined as "problems" in the first place.[16] Morozov calls this "solutionism," and it runs through the tech sector's characteristic desire to solve two problems: to connect people, and to make everyday things easier. Adam Greenfield unpacks the latter as the promotion of an "ideology of ease," in which any friction around everyday tasks – and especially shopping – needs to be eliminated.[17] Sidestepping "techlash" (animus toward Big Tech companies), this may come to be applied to non-market activities, such as solving community problems, perhaps at the level of municipal government. But without state power, these initiatives will be more "make-do-and-mend" than real social reform – let alone revolution. This vision is the essence of progressive technocracy: seeking to improve people's lives through technical solutions, skirting the need for political struggle and confrontation.

The combined effect will be a Left that is left defending the political and cultural aspects of the neoliberalism it professed to despise. The historic role of figures like Corbyn and Sanders will have been to inoculate young people from truly radical politics by showing its ostensible impossibility. The consequence will be to justify the transition of their parties to a position that looks, as far as possible, to preclude mass participation in decision-making processes. Sovereign, national politics – which neoliberalism was designed to defang – will remain beyond the grasp of the Left. Progressives will prefer instead to operate at the municipal, the everyday or the supranational level – precisely the arena to which neoliberalism sought to displace politics, to where it could do no harm.

Finally, the paradoxical position of having a "Left" defending neoliberalism will be justified through reference to the threat of fascism. The fascism of early twentieth century Europe has been consigned to the dustbin of history. As Marxists from Trotsky to Gramsci realized, a key precondition for fascism is a revolutionary threat to the bourgeoisie, the specter of the working-class power – something not present today. Anti-fascism in the 2020s will seize on the center's drift toward greater nationalism (and, indeed, on elements of working-class support for this move) to argue, wrongly, that fascism is back. Organicist far-right politics – on which more below – will also seem to bolster the Left's alarmist case. The purpose of this "anti-fascism" is purely ethical: it gives meaning, urgency and moral legitimacy to the Left, no matter whom they are against or whoever's interests are being served. The post-neoliberal conservatism that is likely to be dominant in the next decade is not a fascist project, however nationalist or authoritarian its inflections. Christophe Guilluy argues that anti-fascism today is at base a class weapon used by the professional-managerial class against the working class, as a way to discredit working-class demands wholesale, independently of their actual content. As he puts it in a particularly uncompromising passage, "[t]he target of today's fashionable antifascism...is the working class, which must be tarred with fascism in order to discredit the complaints of a lower [class]...infected by the disease of 'populism.'"[18] The political upshot will be perpetual attempts to build a "popular front" between liberals, the Left and even some conservatives – delaying the task of building radical, independent working-class politics.

8.4 Authoritarian Populism: the Far-Right

Frightening reactionary politics will continue to emerge, however. The extent of this, though, will depend on the success (or lack thereof) of mainstream politics' incorporation of sections of the masses in a new national project, and their absorption of anti-political energies. If the new nationalist Center is unable to appease anti-establishment revolt – and if the Left is unable to give voice to it – then far-right politics will profit. It may be that the US Alt-Right described in Angela Nagle's *Kill All Normies* is by now exhausted, its transgressivism spent. But there will continue to be alienated young people (and especially young men) in the US and beyond, who could seek to politicize white (and male?) identity.

Instead, the continuing void of political authority may well lead the Far-Right to rally around the need for a "great personality" or strongman who presents themselves as the solution to the drift of the political moment, or as the savior or redeemer of the nation – especially in a US in terminal decline. This twenty-first century strongman populism seizes on the hollowness of political authority and tries to substitute for it with direct force. If a section of the population interprets the breakdown of neoliberalism as due to a *surfeit* of democracy (interpreted as either representative institutions or counter-majoritarian institutions), rather than due to a *deficit,* then authoritarian politics will have traction. Brazil's trajectory in the late 2010s – explored in Chapter 5 – provides a template, where the populist incorporation of widespread anti-political sentiment led to Bolsonaro's election.[19] If the neoliberal state is "hard but hollow," then the Far-Right's solution to political intractability and drift is to dial up the "hard" part.

Another development may involve a confluence between xenophobia and Malthusian conceptions. Already visible are certain reactionary and anti-humanist strands in green politics, with a distinctively austere and anti-immigrant shade. When faced with a global pandemic, one line of thinking has been to play up the catastrophic elements, blaming humans as the virus and celebrating nature's revenge. A nationalist interpretation would see a forceful rejection of globalization and cosmopolitanism: the organic body of the indigenous nation is threatened by deleterious outside influences, and limits on resources necessitate their exclusion. Austria already has a coalition between the conservative Right and Greens, for instance. Widespread and growing ecological consciousness may meet existing right-wing populist politics, especially in places like Germany or Switzerland. Of course, ecology – like concern with identity – has always been a reactionary tradition. The coming period will see them return to their natural home on the Right, after a half-century under the wing of the New Left.

Across the Right, then, the next decade is likely to manifest a combination of reformist and reactionary responses to the breakdown of neoliberalism. Of these, a post-neoliberal conservatism seems to offer the most viable model for a short-term hegemonic project with the least disruption. This appears plausible in the most consolidated democracies, such as the UK. Elsewhere, the boundaries between the Far-Right and the Center-Right may be more blurry and the situation less stable. In the European periphery – and indeed the global semi-periphery – more authoritarian outcomes are likely; and they may involve the continuation of punitive neoliberal policies.

What is important to note, though, is that if a new hegemony is achieved, it will be based not on the strength of the vision, but rather on the weakness of Left opposition. This weakness will persist so long as the Left is rooted in "moral minoritarianism" (a preference for moral arguments rather than building political projects designed to win power through majoritarian decision-making processes). If the Right achieves hegemony, then, it will be a *conditional hegemony*, dependent on the weakness of the Left.

8.5 Despair not

The ideological map of the next decade will be determined by the extent to which the Center is able to incorporate and respond to anti-politics, and provide new conditions for capital accumulation. It will try to do so by advancing a model of state-capitalism. The institutional Left, by embracing progressive technocracy, will possibly become the most vocal defender of some aspects of the status quo ante. Its position with regard to the new Center will be as moral and technical critic; its response to the Far-Right will be to try to create a popular front. On the Far-Right, a range of different reactionary responses to the breakdown of neoliberalism seem possible, which will all demand more heavy-handed state action (be it at the borders or within society), as a response to the weak authority of the Center.

We should be clear that this is no cause for despair among socialists. The defeat of left-populism and the final death of social democracy represent a chance for a movement that aims to build working-class self-government. Notwithstanding the extraordinary counter-crisis responses we have just seen, global capitalism remains stagnant. Just as neoliberalism provided an inadequate solution to the crisis of the 1970s, so whatever emerges next will not fully resolve the crises of the 2010s. As we've explored, the Center-Right will not have new ideas but rather serve-up a reheated corporatism. Now that older models have failed, perhaps there is an opening for a new socialism at the End of the End of History.

Chapter 9

Conclusion

The End of History truly felt as if it would be forever. But the fact it crumbled so rapidly and with such little genuine organized opposition indicated how fragile it had become. The first economic blow came in the wake of the Global Financial Crisis of 2008, the political blow in 2016, and its final collapse in 2020. All of this has been accelerated by the Covid-19 pandemic that disintegrated precisely those institutions that had helped to justify or shore up the status quo ante: just-in-time supply chains, justified in terms of their efficiency, snapped, leading to shortages, exacerbating pandemic hoarding. Production outsourced to East Asia left states with hollowed-out industrial capacity and the inability to maintain basic health infrastructure, while public health systems had been steadily degraded, drained of resources as they were marketized. Labor market flexibility, justified on the grounds of nimble adaptiveness, exacerbated labor market collapse and mass unemployment, precipitating the wholescale implosion of the US labor market. It is difficult to understate the terrible costs of responses to the pandemic – not only the lethal consequences of mismanagement on the basis of poor, uneven and conflicting data, but also the tremendous mangling of civil liberty through rolling lockdowns and states of emergency and – worse in the long run – calamitous economic collapse.

The result has been a low-grade dystopia. Throughout the Western world, the Left has braced for far-right revival led by authoritarian, charismatic demagogues such as Donald Trump and Boris Johnson, who would degrade constitutional order and inflate nationalist passions to entrench their personal power. As liberal order crumbled away, we do indeed have a dystopia appropriate to our times – although not the one we were expecting. Donald Trump, styled for so long as a would-be fascist dictator by so much of the Left, has not used the occasion of an unprecedented public health crisis as his "Reichstag" moment to seize dictatorial power by extending the state of emergency. Indeed, the only Western leader to have ruthlessly exploited the lockdown to enhance his personal power is liberal strongman and centrist darling Emmanuel Macron, who used emergency laws that he had already strengthened in order to extend and consolidate his strongman image, while at the same time shifting toward a more explicitly Gaullist and nationalist politics.

In Britain, Boris Johnson, cast by so much of the intelligentsia as the populist lord of misrule, retreated behind committees of scientists, technocrats and experts that he and his allies had hitherto lambasted in their ascent to power. Unsurprisingly, the result was chaotic, as experts disagreed among themselves in the midst of confronting a pandemic caused by a new and poorly understood virus. With the abdication of British leadership before Covid-19, we saw the last flare-up of technocratic rule – even as it disintegrated into warring academic factions based on competing methodologies, assumptions and models. The unsustainability of technocracy as a mode of governance was plainly revealed in the unevenness and mismanagement of lockdown policies across the Western world.

If the new coronavirus destroyed the legitimacy of technocracy, it also consummated the destruction of left-populist revolt at the ballot box. As we have seen throughout the book, left-populism disintegrated or confronted its limits in various votes – Senator Bernie Sanders' capitulation to Joe Biden in the 2020 Democratic primaries, Syriza's election defeat in 2019 following their surrender to the EU in 2015, Corbyn's defeat to Johnson's Tories in 2019 following his embrace of a second referendum, Podemos' slouching into an alliance with Spain's tired old Socialist Party...

Covid-19 has completed this process, compressing what would otherwise have been a more tortuous process of decline. This was most evident in the emergency economic policies launched by governments to respond to collapsing consumption and investment, itself pre-empted by government responses to the virus: a Trumpian UBI in the US and a revival of emergency Cold War-era industrial policy. In the UK, the state not only surreptitiously nationalized the railways – long a Labour Party aspiration – but nationalized most of Britain's wage bill to boot.

The rapidity with which governments that had been castigated as far-right and market fundamentalist drew on state capacity and resources to manage the pandemic and drastically demobilize the economy is particularly striking. Needless to say, little of this is meaningfully progressive in any real sense of the term, not to mention corrupt, halting and uneven. Doubtless, there will be political disputes over restoring normalcy and how to deal with the resulting spikes in state borrowing and spending. Yet, while left-populists can pathetically claim retrospective vindication for their favored economic policies, they can no longer offer any distinctive alternative to the Right, which has now already assimilated the political terrain of *dirigisme* while the free market dogmas – always honored in the breach more than the observance – crumble away. Social democrats and left-populists can now offer themselves as better managers of a new political-economic order, but the collapse of their distinctive appeal forces them back onto the technocratic ground of offering themselves as more effective managers of this new dispensation, with perhaps extra protections and pay-offs for the vulnerable.

The Covid-19 pandemic completed the dissolution of the End of History regime, and the immediate result was a cozy dystopia for the left intelligentsia: a drastic escalation of state power and coercion and the state-directed collapse of capitalist market mechanisms, with the middle classes confined to home, whether working remotely or furloughed. The working classes meanwhile – at least those in sectors such as delivery, cooking, food processing, agriculture, health and care and so on – were compelled to continue working. Despite the costs of the pandemic – deaths, suffering, curtailed civil liberties and economic collapse – there is the possibility that the pandemic could stoke a revival of popular politics, and perhaps even working-class politics. What is striking about the moment is that even while states demobilized whole regions and countries in their efforts to slow the spread of the virus, they were at the same time forced to implicate and involve their constituents, citizens and voters in ways that are new: state propaganda around the lockdown enjoined all citizens in collective responsibility for public health, and collective participation in protecting social interests.

It is, to be sure, a minimal and hedged form of national politics, a truncated embodiment of collective responsibility – "stay home" as per the message of so many governments. The form of this collective vision notwithstanding, the content is different to the persistent efforts of the past to shrink and strangle the public sphere over the last 3 decades, in which the public have been repelled from collective life, with the result that social order has been entrusted to lawyers, activists, remote governmental experts on transnational commissions, central bankers, technocrats, the market, CEOs...not to ordinary citizens. Unsurprisingly, this era coincided with the age of the consumer – the privatized, apathetic citizen-voter, encouraged to benefit from low inflation and cheap goods resulting from global trade and supply chains, and to consume politics, in turn, as a remote, mediatized spectacle offering different brands of essentially similar products, while not concerning themselves with the questions of how production functions, is organized or distributed. That was left to the supply chain managers, investors and trade negotiators, not unions or politicians. That dirty, menial, lowly working-class jobs have been thrust into public consciousness as "essential" suggests that society might be forced to consider questions of production afresh.

Finally, out of all the misery associated with the pandemic, there were some heartening moments that indicated the possibility of renewed political consciousness on the part of workers for their distinctive interests as producers. In a stroke, the pandemic scrambled the de facto labor hierarchy that had prevailed over the last 30 years, which privileged CEOs, bond traders, entrepreneurs, financiers and middle-class professionals. Society's continued dependence on "essential" – i.e., working class – labor has been exposed. In some places, workers even spontaneously retooled their factories to manufacture medical machinery while in others, workers revolted against cramped and unsanitary working conditions in the midst of the pandemic. While the middle classes were freed to cower at home and oligarchs saw their assets spontaneously expand as a result of state efforts to keep the economy on life support, workers were forced to work. Perhaps workers – and others – will come to a greater appreciation of their own agency, not only in sustaining the economy but in maintaining society itself. The limit here is, of course, that expressions of worker solidarity and self-interest were cast in terms of protection from the virus, not assuming control of society itself. Were politics to be rooted once again in the self-interest of producers, the will to self-rule must overcome the politics of fear on which the Covid-19 pandemic thrives. Thus, in the midst of all the confusion, fragmentation and hysteria – at the End of the End of History, there are still grounds for hope and confidence.

Endnotes

Chapter 1

1. To cite just a few 2016 obits: Garry Shandling, Leonard Cohen, Florence Henderson, David Bowie, Muhammad Ali, John Glenn, George Michael, Alan Rickman, Prince, Gene Wilder, Zsa Zsa Gabor. Although some of these are of the "Silent Generation," the point is that the disappearance of icons of Cold War popular culture seemed to say something about the passing of a moment in the West.

2. The exception here may be Greece, where there was significant mass mobilization, which bolstered Syriza in government.

3 Hobsbawm, Eric. *The Age of Extremes: The Short Twentieth Century, 1914-1991*. London: Abacus, 2011. p. 562.

4. *Ibid.* p. 563.

5. In the *Century of the Self*, a four-part documentary, Adam Curtis sought to examine the connections between the Freudian focus on inner life and the psyche, and the growth of public relations and advertising. The title referred to the twentieth century, but it was truly at the century's end that "the self" – especially the consuming self – came to reign unchallenged.

6. Cross, Gary S. *An All-Consuming Century: Why Commercialism Won in Modern America*. Columbia University Press, 2000.

7. Maren Thom (/100/ What Was the End of History?), *Aufhebunga Bunga* (podcast). December 10, 2019. https://aufhebungabunga.podbean.com/e/100-what-was-the-end-of-history-ft-many-guests/.

8. Fisher, Mark. *Capitalist Realism: Is There No Alternative?* Winchester, UK: Zero Books, 2010.

9. Calcutt, Andrew. *Arrested Development: Pop Culture and the Erosion of Adulthood*. London, UK: Continuum, 2000. Greil

Marcus cited therein.

10. Fisher, Mark. *Capitalist Realism: Is There No Alternative?* Winchester, UK: Zero Books, 2010.
See also: Aufhebunga Bunga (/46/ Exiting Capitalist Realism), *Aufhebunga Bunga* (podcast). August 30, 2018. https://aufhebungabunga.podbean.com/e/46-exiting-capitalist-realism/.

11. Ballard, J.G. *Cocaine Nights*. London: Flamingo, 1996.
See also: Simon Sellars (/109/ Bunga Goes Ballard), *Aufhebunga Bunga* (podcast). February 25, 2020. https://aufhebungabunga. podbean.com/e/109-bunga-goes-ballard-ft-simon-sellars/.

12. Catherine Liu (/37/ The Ghosts of May '68, *Aufhebunga Bunga* (podcast). May 16, 2018. https://aufhebungabunga. podbean.com/e/37-the-ghosts-of-may-68-ft-catherine-liu/

13. Boltanski, Luc, and Eve Chiapello. *The New Spirit of Capitalism*. Translated by Gregory Elliott. London: Verso, 2018. See also: Hochuli, Alex. "Is Contemporary Anti-Consumerism a Form of Romantic Anti-Capitalism?" 2008. https://www.academia.edu/32436755/Is_contemporary_anti-consumerism_a_form_of_romantic_anti-capitalism

14. Reynolds, Simon. *Retromania: Pop Cultures Addiction to Its Own Past*. London: Faber, 2012.

15. In a bizarre rerun, the environmentalist "Extinction Rebellion," that has emerged in recent years, re-enacts the same tropes of over a decade earlier, as if the 2000s had never happened.
See: Leigh Phillips (/91/ Exhaustion Revealing), *Aufhebunga Bunga* (podcast). October 10, 2019. https://aufhebungabunga. podbean.com/e/91-exhaustion-revealing-ft-leigh-phillips/

16. Alex Hochuli (/47/ Woke Consumerism), *Aufhebunga Bunga* (podcast). September 13, 2018. https://aufhebungabunga. podbean.com/e/47-woke-consumerism/.

17. When the Soviet Union announced itself as a formidable technological and military rival to the US. See: Milanovic,

Branko. "Is the Pandemic China's Sputnik Moment?" Foreign Affairs, May 13, 2020. https://www.foreignaffairs.com/articles/united-states/2020-05-12/pandemic-chinas-sputnik-moment.

18. One might add that Iraq exceeded Eastern Europe in the force by which the implantation of liberal democracy was attempted. And (by coincidence?) Iraq today sees significant mass anti-corruption protest.

Chapter 2

1. Fukuyama, Francis. "The End of History?" *The National Interest*, no. 16 (Summer 1989): 3-18. doi:https://www.jstor.org/stable/24027184.

2. Indeed, the Cold War would come to you even if you didn't want it. Those countries that staked a claim for an independent path of development quickly ended up – by attraction via enticements, or by violent repulsion – in the arms of one or other camp.
   See: Vincent Bevins. (/121/ Those Murdering Bastards), *Aufhebunga Bunga* (podcast), May 5, 2020. https://aufhebungabunga.podbean.com/e/121-those-murdering-bastards-ft-vincent-bevins/.

3. See Fukuyama's later books, notably *Political Order and Political Decay: From the Industrial Revolution to the Globalisation of Democracy*. New York: Farrar, Straus and Giroux, 2015.

4. Fukuyama, Francis. *The End of History and the Last Man*. New York, N.Y: Free Press, 1992.

5. Mandelson was specifically referring to the voters of South Wales, but the point is a general one.
   Cited in O'Hagan, Ellie Mae. "A political earthquake – that's what it takes for the press to notice Wales," The Guardian. April 26, 2017. https://www.theguardian.com/commentisfree/2017/apr/26/press-wales-labour-meltdown-

heartland.

6. This section draws on the work of Adam Tooze. See: *Crashed: How a Decade of Financial Crisis Changed the World.* Westminster: Penguin Publishing Group, 2018.

7. Bickerton, Chris. "Labour's Lost Working-class Voters Have Gone for Good." The Guardian. December 19, 2019. https://www.theguardian.com/commentisfree/2019/dec/19/labour-working-class-voters-brexit.

8. Zakaria, Fareed. "The End of The End of History." Newsweek. September 23, 2001. https://www.newsweek.com/end-end-history-152075.

9. Kagan, Robert, *The Return of History and the End of Dreams,* London: Atlantic Books, 2009.
Gat, Azar, "The Return of Authoritarian Great Powers." Foreign Affairs. July/August, 2007. https://www.foreignaffairs.com/articles/china/2007-07-01/return-authoritarian-great-powers.

10. Jacoby, Russell. *The End of Utopia: Politics and Culture in an Age of Apathy.* New York: Basic Books, 2000.

11. This section draws on Todd McGowan's book on Hegel, *Emancipation after Hegel: Achieving a Contradictory Revolution.* New York: Columbia University Press, 2019.

Chapter 3

1. The words are those of the first permanent President of the European Council (2009-14), Herman Von Rompoy. Cited in Jäger, Anton. "The Myth of 'Populism.'" Jacobin, March 1, 2018. https://jacobinmag.com/2018/01/populism-douglas-hofstadter-donald-trump-democracy.

2. For an account of the anti-democratic and anti-popular uses to which "populism" is put, see: D'Eramo, Marco, "Populism and the New Oligarchy," NLR 82, July-August 2013." https://newleftreview.org/issues/II82/articles/marco-d-eramo-populism-and-the-new-oligarchy.

3. Hochuli, Alex. "Technocracy's End-of-Life Rally." Damage. May 8, 2020. https://damagemag.com/2020/05/08/technocracys-end-of-life-rally/.

4. Schlesinger, Arthur, Jr. "It's My 'Vital Center'." Slate Magazine. January 10, 1997. https://slate.com/news-and-politics/1997/01/it-s-my-vital-center.html.

5. Cited in: Siddique, Haroon. "Tony Blair Says Tories and Labour Engaged in 'populism Running Riot'." The Guardian. November 25, 2019. https://www.theguardian.com/politics/2019/nov/25/tony-blair-tories-labour-populism-election.

6. Mudde mischaracterizes the "general will" – it is better understood as the precondition for pluralism, rather than its opposite. See Rousseau, Jean-Jacques, *The Social Contract*. London: Penguin, 2006.
    Mudde, Cass. "Populism in the Twenty-First Century: An Illiberal Democratic Response to Undemocratic Liberalism," The Andrea Mitchell Center for the Study of Democracy. https://www.sas.upenn.edu/andrea-mitchell-center/cas-mudde-populism-twenty-first-century.

7. Mudde, Cas, and Cristóbal Rovira Kaltwasser. *Populism: A Very Short Introduction*. New York: Oxford University Press, 2017.

8. This section draws from the only recent systematic study of anti-politics: Clarke, Nick. *The Good Politician: Folk Theories, Political Interaction, and the Rise of Anti-politics*. Cambridge: Cambridge University Press, 2018.

9. For an illustration of the particularities of the "political class," see: Oborne, Peter. *The Triumph of the Political Class*. London: Pocket Books, 2009. For a more recent take, looking at the way centrists have adopted ever more "populist" characteristics, see: Kennedy, Joe. *Authentocrats: Culture, Politics and the New Seriousness*. London: Repeater Books, 2018.

10. Lasch, Christopher. *The Revolt of the Elites: And the Betrayal of Democracy*. New York: W. W. Norton and Company, 1996. pp. 6-7.
    See also: Lasch, Christopher. *The Culture of Narcissism: American Life in an Age of Diminishing Expectations*. New York: Warner Books, 1979.
11. Glaser, Eliane. *Anti-Politics*. London: Repeater, 2018.
12. Gray, Freddy. "How Bloomberg Helps Bernie." The Spectator. November 24, 2019. https://blogs.spectator.co.uk/2019/11/how-bloomberg-helps-bernie/.
    Behr, Rafael. "Our Brexit Limbo Has Given Us Two New Parties, but the Same Old Politics." The Guardian, April 23, 2019. https://www.theguardian.com/commentisfree/2019/apr/23/brexit-limbo-new-parties-politics-insurgent-outsider.
    Eagleton, Terry. "The Government of No One by Ruth Kinna Review – the Rise of Anarchism." The Guardian, August 22, 2019. https://www.theguardian.com/books/2019/aug/22/the-government-of-no-one-by-ruth-kinna-review-anarchism.
    Maguire, Patrick. "Robert Kilroy-Silk: The Godfather of Brexit." The New Statesman, September 18, 2019. https://www.newstatesman.com/politics/brexit/2019/09/robert-kilroy-silk-godfather-brexit.
13. Smyth, Sam. "Goofy New Millennium Meets '60s Radical Chic." *Sunday Tribune*, May 7, 2000.
    Righter, Rosemary. "Third Time's a Charm as Berlusconi Gets His Wish." *Irish Independent*, April 16, 2008.
    Plus Ça Change. Transcript. BBC Radio 4. April 01, 2007. http://www.bbc.co.uk/radio4/transcripts/plus_ca_change2.rtf
14. For this conceptualization, see Schedler, Andreas. *The End of Politics?: Explorations into Modern Antipolitics*. Houndmills: Macmillan, 1997.

15. Crouch, Colin, *Post-Democracy*, London: Polity, 2004.
16. This reading of politics draws from the work of French philosopher Jacques Rancière.
    See: Rancière, Jacques. *Disagreement: Politics and Philosophy*. Minneapolis: Univ. of Minnesota Press, 2008.
    Rancière, Jacques. *On the Shores of Politics*. London: Verso, 2006.
    Rancière, Jacques. *Hatred of Democracy*. Translated by Steve Corcoran. London: Verso, 2014.
17. Zizek, Slavoj, "For a leftist appropriation of the European legacy," *Journal of Political Ideologies*, 3:1, 63-78, 1998, DOI: 10.1080/13569319808420769.
18. Rancière, Jacques. *On the Shores of Politics*. London: Verso, 2006. p. 22.
19. Of course, in the Third World, politics rarely took place within a liberal-democratic container. Attempts to play the institutional game, by socialists or nationalists, were often violently crushed, such as in Indonesia in 1965 or Chile in 1973; and popular politics outside institutions rarely succeeded in forcing national institutions to become more representative. Even in the First World, there was plenty of violent, covert and extra-legal activity that prevented politics playing out freely, such as secret networks dedicated to preventing Communist parties from ever winning elections.
20. Crouch, Colin, *Post-Democracy*, London: Polity, 2004.
21. Ince, Anthony, David Featherstone, Andrew Cumbers, Danny Mackinnon, and Kendra Strauss. "British Jobs for British Workers? Negotiating Work, Nation, and Globalisation through the Lindsey Oil Refinery Disputes." *Antipode* 47, no. 1 (2014): 139-57. doi:10.1111/anti.12099.
22. Barrow, Becky. "'British Jobs for British Workers': Brown's Big Lie as Wildcat Strikes Spread over Foreign Labour Shipped into the UK." Daily Mail Online, January 31, 2009. https://www.dailymail.co.uk/news/article-1131708/British-

jobs-British-workers-Wildcat-strikes-spread-foreign-workers-shipped-UK.html.

23. Streeck, Wolfgang. "The Return of the Repressed," New Left Review, March/April 2017. https://newleftreview.org/issues/II104/articles/wolfgang-streeck-the-return-of-the-repressed.

24. Mallet, Victor, and Roula Khalaf. "FT Interview: Emmanuel Macron Says It Is Time to Think the Unthinkable." Financial Times, April 16, 2020. https://www.ft.com/content/3ea8d790-7fd1-11ea-8fdb-7ec06edeef84.

25. Clarke, Nick. *The Good Politician: Folk Theories, Political Interaction, and the Rise of Anti-politics*. Cambridge: Cambridge University Press, 2018. pp. 21-4.

Chapter 4

1. For a summary, see Barkan, Ross. "Will Rachel Maddow Face a Reckoning for Her Trump-Russia Coverage?" The Guardian, March 28, 2019. https://www.theguardian.com/commentisfree/2019/mar/28/trump-russia-investigation-mueller-liberal-media-rachel-maddow.

2. Examples abound. For instance, one news site invited a top commercial lawyer to explain "No-Deal Brexit" through the lens of children's novels and films. Telford, William. "Expert Explains No-deal Brexit by Likening It to Harry Potter." Business Live, June 20, 2019. https://www.business-live.co.uk/economic-development/expert-explains-no-deal-brexit-16455721.

3. If NOBS is not an acronym to your taste, similar formulations include Neoliberal Undoing Terminal Syndrome (NUTS), Paranoia at the End of Neoliberalism Syndrome (PENOS), Postmodern Liberal Establishment Breakdown Syndrome (PLEBS) and Breakdown of Liberal Establishment Hysteria (BLEH). The difficulty in naming 'NOBS' is perhaps a sign that the old ways of analyzing politics are dying, while the

new are only just being born.

4. For instance, the way it purports to be democratic, but cannot countenance mass participation, or how its emphasis on social peace obscures the violence needed to maintain it. See: Aufhebunga Bunga (/45/ Liberalism: A Counter-Podcast), *Aufhebunga Bunga* (podcast), August 16, 2018. https://aufhebungabunga.podbean.com/e/45-liberalism-a-counter-podcast/.

5. Wimmer, Alexander. "Die Linke." The Full Brexit, December 13, 2019. https://www.thefullbrexit.com/die-linke.

6. Krauthammer, Charles, "The Delusional Dean," *Washington Post,* December 5, 2003. https://www.washingtonpost.com/archive/opinions/2003/12/05/the-delusional-dean/cbc80426-08ee-40fd-97e5-19da55fdc821/.

7. Alexander, Harriet. "George W Bush's Book of Paintings Praised by Art Critic and Tops Bestseller List." The Telegraph, March 12, 2017. https://www.telegraph.co.uk/news/2017/03/12/george-w-bushs-book-paintings-praised-art-critic-tops-bestseller/.

8. Any similarity with Theodor Adorno's symptoms of "authoritarian personality" is purely coincidental.

9. For more on the notion of common sense as used here, see: Hoare, George and Nathan Sperber, *An Introduction to Antonio Gramsci: His Life, Thought, and Legacy*, London: Bloomsbury, 2016, Chapter 4.

10. A tweet, subsequently deleted, but saved for posterity in Jones, Owen. "How Online Abuse Is Politically Hijacked." Medium, July 14, 2017. https://medium.com/@OwenJones84/how-online-abuse-is-politically-hijacked-ca27cc62ddf3.

11. Freeman, Hadley. "From Labour's Hard Left to Donald Trump, It's Been the Summer of the Personality Cult." The Guardian, July 30, 2016. https://www.theguardian.com/us-news/2016/jul/30/donald-trump-labour-personality-cult-hadley-freeman.

Johnston, John. "Tony Blair Savages Jeremy Corbyn for Turning Labour into a 'glorified Protest Group with Cult Trimmings.'" Politics Home, February 25, 2020. https://www.politicshome.com/news/uk/political-parties/labour-party/news/108655/tony-blair-savages-jeremy-corbyn-turning-labour.

Stewart, Heather. "Former Minister Quits Labour after 45 Years Blaming 'Corbyn Cult'." The Guardian. May 14, 2019. https://www.theguardian.com/politics/2019/may/14/former-labour-mp-bridget-prentice-quits-party-after-45-years-blaming-corbyn-cult.

12. Morrison, Toni. "On the First Black President." The New Yorker, September 28, 1998. https://www.newyorker.com/magazine/1998/10/05/comment-6543.

13. Krol, Charlotte. "The Justin Trudeau Effect: Famous Faces Who Have Fallen for the Canadian Prime Minister's Charm." The Telegraph, February 17, 2017. https://www.telegraph.co.uk/news/2017/02/17/justin-trudeau-effect-famous-faces-have-fallen-canadian-prime/.

14. Summers, Lawrence H. "How to Fix Globalization-for Detroit, Not Davos." The American Interest, May 27, 2020. https://www.the-american-interest.com/2020/05/22/how-to-fix-globalization-for-detroit-not-davos/.

15. Pincus-Roth, Zachary. "'It's the President We All Want': The Melancholy World of Liberals Watching 'The West Wing' in 2018." The Washington Post, July 20, 2018. https://www.washingtonpost.com/entertainment/tv/in-the-trump-era-some-find-escapism-in-the-west-wing-its-the-president-we-all-want/2018/07/19/05c40fd4-89bb-11e8-85ae-511bc1146b0b_story.html.

16. Michallon, Clémence. "12 West Wing Episodes That Are Ultimate Therapy for the Trump Era." The Independent, September 22, 2019. https://www.independent.co.uk/arts-entertainment/tv/features/west-wing-episodes-best-

donald-trump-cast-white-house-josiah-bartlet-a8627181.
html.

17. Ross, Chuck. "Susan Rice Claims Without Evidence That Russia Could Be Funding Riots." The Daily Caller, May 31, 2020. https://dailycaller.com/2020/05/31/susan-rice-russia-riots-george-floyd-protests/.

18. Rubin, Jennifer. "Trump's Subservience to Putin on Display." The Washington Post, August 27, 2019. https://www.washingtonpost.com/opinions/2019/08/27/trumps-subservience-putin-display/.

19. See for instance: Hirsh, Michael. "Why Putin Is Smiling." Foreign Policy, December 10, 2019. https://foreignpolicy.com/2019/12/10/russia-putin-trump-impeachment-dysfunction-smiling/.

20. Robinson, Nathan J. "The Clinton Comedy of Errors." Current Affairs, April 26, 2017. https://www.currentaffairs.org/2017/04/the-clinton-comedy-of-errors.

21. Jurkowitz, Mark, Amy Mitchell, Elisa Shearer and Mason Walker. "US Media Polarization and the 2020 Election: A Nation Divided." Pew Research Center's Journalism Project. January 24, 2020. https://www.journalism.org/2020/01/24/u-s-media-polarization-and-the-2020-election-a-nation-divided/.

22. "'Post-truth' Declared Word of the Year by Oxford Dictionaries." BBC News, November 16, 2016. https://www.bbc.co.uk/news/uk-37995600.
"Dealing with post-truth politics: 'Postfaktisch' is Germany's Word of the Year." DW, December 9, 2016. https://www.dw.com/en/dealing-with-post-truth-politics-postfaktisch-is-germanys-word-of-the-year/a-36702430.

23. Goodhart, David. "3 New Books Exploring Post-truth." Evening Standard, May 11, 2017. https://www.standard.co.uk/lifestyle/books/3-new-books-exploring-posttruth-a3536521.html.

Block, David. *Post-truth and Political Discourse*. Cham, Switzerland: Palgrave Macmillan, 2019.

24. Mohan, Megha. "Macron Leaks: The Anatomy of a Hack." BBC News, May 09, 2017. https://www.bbc.co.uk/news/blogs-trending-39845105.

25. For instance, see: Brennan, Jason, *Against Democracy*, London: Princeton University Press, 2017.

26. The Independent Group was a short-lived centrist off-shoot from the three main parties in Britain, formed in the belief that there was a large pool of centrist pro-EU voters, for which no other party catered. It failed miserably in the 2019 General Election and was soon after disbanded.
"Pro-Brexit Protestors Sentenced after Abusing Anna Soubry MP." Crown Prosecution Service, July 29, 2019. https://www.cps.gov.uk/london-south/news/pro-brexit-protestors-sentenced-after-abusing-anna-soubry-mp.

27. Deboick, Sophia. "A YEAR IN MUSIC: 2012, Britain before the Fall." The New European, February 13, 2019. https://www.theneweuropean.co.uk/top-stories/a-year-in-music-2012-britain-before-the-fall-1-5883381.

28. Katie Couric, Twitter post, May 29, 2020, 3 pm, https://twitter.com/katiecouric/status/1266429206633857024.

29. Garry Kasparov, Twitter post, July 16, 2018, 1.20 pm, https://twitter.com/kasparov63/status/1018893198058573824.

30. O'Carroll, Lisa, Jessica Elgot and Denis Campbell. "Brexit Threat to School Dinners Comes as Stockpiling Intensifies." The Guardian, January 31, 2019. https://www.theguardian.com/politics/2019/jan/31/progress-on-school-dinners-could-be-rewound-after-brexit.
Wharton, Jane. "England's Top Medical Chief Warns of Deaths after No-deal Brexit." Metro, November 15, 2019. https://metro.co.uk/2019/10/10/englands-top-medical-chief-warns-deaths-no-deal-brexit-10895809/.
"EU Withdrawal Scenarios and Monetary and Financial

Stability." Bank of England, November 28, 2018. https://www.bankofengland.co.uk/report/2018/eu-withdrawal-scenarios-and-monetary-and-financial-stability.

Butler, Sarah. "Greggs to Stockpile Bacon and Tuna to Avert Brexit Shortages." The Guardian, October 1, 2019. https://www.theguardian.com/business/2019/oct/01/greggs-to-stockpile-bacon-and-tuna-to-avert-brexit-shortages.

City & Finance Reporter for the Daily Mail. "Brexit Raspberry Fears: Ocado Warns of Shortages If There Is No Deal." This Is Money, September 17, 2019. https://www.thisismoney.co.uk/money/markets/article-7474983/Brexit-raspberry-mozzarella-fears-Ocado-bosses-warn-shortages-No-Deal.html.

31. Quinn, RJ. "Politics Is Not Harry Potter." Jacobin, January 4, 2019. https://www.jacobinmag.com/2019/01/harry-potter-magic-liberalism-fantasy-fetishism.

32. Penny, Laurie. "I Want My Country Back." June 24, 2016. https://www.newstatesman.com/politics/uk/2016/06/i-want-my-country-back.

Paul Mason. Twitter post, December 12, 2019, 7:06 pm, https://twitter.com/paulmasonnews/status/1205247632135872516.

33. "Clinton: Half of Trump Supporters 'basket of Deplorables.'" BBC News. September 10, 2016. https://www.bbc.com/news/av/election-us-2016-37329812/clinton-half-of-trump-supporters-basket-of-deplorables.

34. Kirby, Alan. *Digimodernism: How New Technologies Dismantle the Postmodern and Reconfigure our Culture*, New York: Continnum, 2009.

Maren Thom, using a metaphor drawn from social media, calls this "the endless scrolling of cinema." (/106/ The Endless Scrolling of Cinema), *Aufhebunga Bunga* (podcast), February 4, 2020. https://www.patreon.com/posts/106-endless-of-33718402.

35. Andeweg, Rudy. "Political recruitment and party

government" in: *The Nature of Party Government: A Comparative European Perspective*, edited by Jean Blondel and Maurizio Cotta, Basingstoke: Palgrave: 2000, p. 140.

36. Frost, Amber A'Lee. "The Necessity of Political Vulgarity." Current Affairs, August 25, 2016. https://www.currentaffairs. org/2016/05/the-necessity-of-political-vulgarity.

37. Hoare, George. "The Left Against the People?" Brave New Europe, December 13, 2018. https://braveneweurope.com/ george-hoare-the-left-against-the-people.

Chapter 5

1. Hochuli, Alex. "Technocracy's End-of-Life Rally." Damage, May 8, 2020. https://damagemag.com/2020/05/08/ technocracys-end-of-life-rally/.

2. Johnson, Keith. "2019: A Year of Global Protest." Foreign Policy, December 23, 2019. https://foreignpolicy. com/2019/12/23/2019-a-year-of-global-protest/.

3. "Do Today's Global Protests Have Anything in Common?" BBC News. BBC, November 11, 2019. https://www.bbc.com/ news/world-50123743.

4. Formerly the Lega Nord – a populist, xenophobic and regionalist party based in the north of Italy – the party rebranded as just the Lega in 2018, dropping the regionalist emphasis to become a nationwide right-wing populist party.

5. Dunn, Elizabeth. "Audit, Corruption, And the Problem of Personhood: Scenes from Postsocialist Poland." Lecture at Wissenchaftskolleg, Berlin, 1999. Cited in Krastev, Ivan. *Shifting Obsessions Three Essays on the Politics of Anticorruption*. Budapest: Central European University Press, 2004.

6. Abăseacă, Raluca. "#Rezist. Citizens Are Back on the Streets in Romania." openDemocracy, February 15, 2017. https:// www.opendemocracy.net/en/can-europe-make-it/rezist-citizens-are-back-on-streets-in-romania/

7. Adi, Ana G, and Darren G Lilleker, eds. *#Rezist – Romania's*

2017 Anti-Corruption Protests: Causes, Development and Implications. Berlin: Quadriga University of Applied Sciences, 2017. http://www.romanianprotests.info/.

8. Indeed, foreign commentators seemed perplexed, describing protests as populist as well as in favor of more rational and efficient government. C.f. Bohl, Ryan. "Romania Rising: Populism by Different Means and without Ugliness." Salon, Salon.com, February 11, 2017. https://www.salon.com/2017/02/12/romania-rising-the-european-countrys-populism-by-different-means_partner/.

9. Cameron, Rob. "Slovakia's Matovic: Europe's Mr Ordinary Prepares for Power," BBC News. BBC, March 4, 2020. https://www.bbc.com/news/world-europe-51718395.

10. Sa'eed Husaini (/61/ Making Plans for Naija), *Aufhebunga Bunga* (podcast), February 14, 2019. https://aufhebungabunga.podbean.com/e/61-making-plans-for-naija-ft-saeed-husaini/.

11. Sean Jacobs (/27/ After Zuma), *Aufhebunga Bunga* (podcast), January 31, 2018. https://aufhebungabunga.podbean.com/e/27-cyrils-south-africa-ft-sean-jacobs/.

12. The point was made specifically about the French Third Republic, but can also be applied more broadly. Gramsci, Antonio. *Selections from the Prison Notebooks.* Translated by Quintin Hoare and Geoffrey Nowell-Smith. New York: International Publishers, 1971, p. 80.

13. For the sake of brevity, we will bookend this narrative with late 2018 and Jair Bolsonaro's election as president.

14. For an account of Brazilian anti-corruption politics, see: Hochuli, Alex. 2017. "The Ends of Lava Jato." Jacobin, December 4, 2017. https://jacobinmag.com/2017/04/brazil-lava-jato-corruption-dilma-rousseff-lula-temer-mani-pulite-italy.

15. Hochuli, Alex. 2018. "Brazil's Anti-Politics Election." Jacobin, July 9, 2018. https://jacobinmag.com/2018/09/brazil-

election-bolsonaro-lula-haddad-boulos-corruption.

16. Krastev, Ivan. 2014. *Democracy Disrupted: the Politics of Global Protest*. Philadelphia: University of Pennsylvania Press.

17. ibid. p. 19.

18. The broad outlines of such a view are expressed in Tad Tietze, Symptomatic Redness (podcast). February 25, 2019. https://www.listennotes.com/podcasts/douglaslaincom/symptomatic-redness-tad-jqFbv8GBd0l/.

19. Glaser, Eliane. *Anti-Politics: on the Demonization of Ideology, Authority and the State*. London: Repeater Books, 2018, p. 84.

20. Cunliffe, Philip. Medium, March 23, 2020. https://medium.com/@thephilippics/are-we-all-covid-communists-now-9825a2067d51.

21. See Chapter 7 for the dangers of mistaking culture war for class polarization.

22. This formulation is taken from Jäger, Anton. "We Bet the House on Left Populism – and Lost." Jacobin, November 25, 2019. https://www.jacobinmag.com/2019/11/we-bet-the-house-on-left-populism-and-lost/.
    See also: Anton Jäger (/120/ Damaged Beyond Repair), *Aufhebunga Bunga* (podcast), May 9, 2020. https://aufhebungabunga.podbean.com/e/unlocked-120-damaged-beyond-repair-ft-anton-jager/.

Chapter 6

1. Ginsborg, Paul. *Silvio Berlusconi: Television, Power and Patrimony*. London: Verso, 2005.

2. Michele Caccavale, cited in: Ginsborg, *op cit.*, p. 69.

3. The so-called "Pact of the Sardines." See: David Broder (/100/ What Was the End of History?), *Aufhebunga Bunga* (podcast), December 10, 2019.
   https://aufhebungabunga.podbean.com/e/100-what-was-the-end-of-history-ft-many-guests/.

4. Weber, Max, *Economy and Society: An Outline of Interpretative*

Sociology. Berkeley: University of California Press, 1978, pp. 1028-9.

5. Ginsborg, *op cit.*

6. The latter was a lie, but little matter, the point was made. It is not hard to imagine Trump making the same performative gesture, eliding the distinction between his private activities and public policies.

7. "Special liberty" is a concept advanced by criminologist Steve Hall, denoting a "sense of entitlement to do what must be done, which is felt by individuals as they actively conform to the systemic logic of the 'business' that will provide them with wealth, enjoyment and personal freedom." "Interview with Prof Steve Hall on Ultra-realist Criminology." Injustice, January 2, 2018. https://www.injustice-film.com/2018/01/02/interview-prof-steve-hall-ultra-realist-criminology/.
See also: Steve Hall (/65/ Bunga Gets Ultra-Real) *Aufhebunga Bunga* (podcast), March 7, 2019. https://aufhebungabunga.podbean.com/e/65-bunga-gets-ultra-real-ft-steve-hall/.

8. The term comes from French political theorist Bernhard Manin. *The Principles of Representative Government.* Cambridge: Cambridge UP, 1997.

9. Ginsborg, *op cit.*, p. 33

10. Mancini, Paolo, *Between Commodification and Lifestyle Politics: Does Silvio Berlusconi Provide a New Model of Politics for the Twenty-first Century?* Oxford: Reuters Institute for the Study of Journalism, 2011.

11. Blokker, Paul, and Manuel Anselmi. "Introduction." In *Multiple Populisms: Italy as Democracy's Mirror*, edited by Paul Blokker and Manuel Anselmi, 1-14. Basingstoke: Routledge, 2019.

12. Della Sala, Vincent. "Hollowing out and Hardening the State: European Integration and the Italian Economy." *West European Politics* 20, no. 1 (1997): 14-33.

doi:10.1080/01402389708425173.

13. For a discussion of the similarities and differences, see: Hochuli, Alex. "The Ends of Lava Jato." Jacobin, April 12, 2017. https://jacobinmag.com/2017/04/brazil-lava-jato-corruption-dilma-rousseff-lula-temer-mani-pulite-italy.

14. D'Emilio, Frances. "Italy's Ex-premier Berlusconi Campaigns against Populism." AP NEWS, February 12, 2018. https://apnews.com/39475e034d844d6eb216612edfba5538/Italy's-ex-premier-Berlusconi-campaigns-against-populism.

Chapter 7

1. For extensive data and analysis on these long-term trends, see: Hay, Colin, *Why We Hate Politics*, Cambridge: Polity, 2007; and Stoker, Gerry, *Why Politics Matters: Making Democracy Work*, London: Palgrave Macmillan, 2006.

2. The Democratic and Republican parties in the US are exceptions in that they have long been cartel parties, in contrast to their European equivalents. Cartel parties are characterized by their collusion, rather than competition, with one another.

3. Mair, Peter. *Ruling the Void: The Hollowing of Western Democracy*. London: Verso, 2013. p. 1.

4. Beppe Grillo, cited in: Bickerton, Christopher J., and Carlo Invernizzi Accetti. "'Techno-populism' as a New Party Family: The Case of the Five Star Movement and Podemos." *Contemporary Italian Politics* 10, no. 2 (May 21, 2018): 132-50. doi:10.1080/23248823.2018.1472919.

5. Paolo Gerbaudo (/60/ Party Time, Online), *Aufhebunga Bunga* (podcast). January 31, 2019. https://aufhebungabunga. podbean.com/e/60-party-time-online-ft-paolo-gerbaudo/.

6. Gerbaudo, Paolo, *The Digital Party: Political Organisation and Online Democracy*, London: Pluto, 2018, p. 315.

7. Bickerton, Chris. "The Five Star Movement and the Rise of 'techno-populist' Parties." LSE EUROPP Blog, June

5, 2018. Accessed May 21, 2020. https://blogs.lse.ac.uk/ europpblog/2018/05/24/the-five-star-movement-and-the- rise-of-techno-populist-parties/.

8. Seymour, Richard. "Bye Bye Labour." London Review of Books, November 7, 2019. https://www.lrb.co.uk/the-paper/ v37/n08/richard-seymour/bye-bye-labour.

9. Kenan Malik (/70/ In Defence of Universalism), Aufhebunga Bunga (podcast). May 2, 2019. https://aufhebungabunga. podbean.com/e/70-in-defence-of-universalism-ft-kenan- malik/.

   For a history of how concern with identity moved from the Right to the Left, and back again, see: Malik, Kenan. "The History and Politics of White Identity." Pandaemonium. March 17, 2019. Accessed May 21, 2020. https://kenanmalik. com/2019/03/16/the-history-and-politics-of-white-identity/.

10. Fraser, Nancy, and Bhaskar Sunkara. *The Old Is Dying and the New Cannot Be Born: From Progressive Neoliberalism to Trump and Beyond*. London: Verso, 2019.

11. All data from "Collective Bargaining in OECD and accession countries," OECD, Paris, September 2017. https://www.oecd. org/els/emp/Industrial-disputes.pdf; except * from "Strikes – Map of Europe." European Trade Union Institute, ETUI. Accessed June 03, 2020. https://www.etui.org/Services/ Strikes-Map-of-Europe/EU-28. "x" denotes missing data.

12. Dahlum, Sirianne, Carl Henrik Knutsen, and Tore Wig. "Who Revolts? Empirically Revisiting the Social Origins of Democracy." *The Journal of Politics* 81, no. 4 (August 30, 2019): 1494-499. doi:10.1086/704699.

13. Giugni, Marco, and Maria T. Grasso. *Street Citizens: Protest Politics and Social Movement Activism in the Age of Globalization*. New York: Cambridge University Press, 2019.

14. Roser, Max, and Esteban Ortiz-Ospina. "Tertiary Education." Our World in Data. July 17, 2013. Accessed May 22, 2020. https://ourworldindata.org/tertiary-education.

"Digest of Education Statistics, 2018." National Center for Education Statistics (NCES) Home Page, a Part of the US Department of Education, 2018. Accessed May 22, 2020. https://nces.ed.gov/programs/digest/d18/tables/dt18_302.60.asp.

"Participation Rates in Higher Education: Academic Years 2006/2007 – 2017/2018." Department for Education, UK. Accessed May 22, 2020. https://assets.publishing.service.gov.uk/government/uploads/system/uploads/attachment_data/file/843542/Publication_HEIPR1718.pdf.

15. Ehrenreich, Barbara, and John Ehrenreich. "The Professional-Managerial Class." *Radical America* 13, no. 2 (March/April 1977): 7-32.

16. *Ibid.* p. 13.

17. Ehrenreich, Barbara, and John Ehrenreich. *Death of a Yuppie Dream: The Rise and Fall of the Professional-Managerial Class.* New York: Rosa Luxemburg Siftung, 2013.

18. Frost, Amber A'Lee. "The Characterless Opportunism of the Managerial Class." American Affairs Journal, November 20, 2019. Accessed May 22, 2020. https://americanaffairsjournal.org/2019/11/the-characterless-opportunism-of-the-managerial-class/.

19. For instance, in 2016 more than 60 percent of white liberals thought the black-white achievement gap was caused by discrimination, a figure that was 42 percent in 2012. This dynamic puts white liberals not only out of sync with the broader population, but even with the minority groups for which they pretend to speak.

See: Goldberg, Zach. "America's White Saviors." Tablet Magazine, June 6, 2019. Accessed May 22, 2020. https://www.tabletmag.com/sections/news/articles/americas-white-saviors.

20. Starr, Terrell Jermaine. "Barbara Smith, Who Helped Coin the Term 'Identity Politics,' Endorses Bernie Sanders." The

Root, February 3, 2020. Accessed May 22, 2020. https://www.theroot.com/barbara-smith-who-helped-coin-the-term-identity-politi-1841419291.

21. Tragically, it may have been Sanders' attempt to respond to these bad-faith criticisms that played a role in tanking his 2020 campaign, a point argued by Angela Nagle and Michael Tracey: (/126/ Mr Bunga Goes to Washington (3)), *Aufhebunga Bunga* (podcast). June 2, 2020. https://aufhebungabunga.podbean.com/e/126-mr-bunga-goes-to-washington-3-ft-angela-nagle-michael-tracey/.

22. Joel Kotkin (/78/ CaliBunga: Tech, Drugs & Capitalist Soul, Pt. 3), *Aufhebunga Bunga* (podcast), July 4, 2019. https://aufhebungabunga.podbean.com/e/78-calibunga-tech-drugs-capitalist-soul-pt-3/.
See also: Kotkin, Joel. *The New Class Conflict.* Candor, NY: Telos Press Publishing, 2014.

23. Lind, Michael. "The New Class War." American Affairs Journal, August 6, 2017. Accessed May 22, 2020. https://americanaffairsjournal.org/2017/05/new-class-war/.

24. Guilluy, Christophe. *Twilight of the Elites: Prosperity, the Periphery, and the Future of France,* London: Yale University Press, 2019.

25. Frost, op. cit.

26. Piketty, Thomas. *Brahmin Left vs Merchant Right: Rising Inequality & the Changing Structure of Political Conflict (Evidence from France, Britain and the US, 1948-2017).* Working paper no. 2018/7. World Inequality Database, 2018.

27. Democrats in the US, Labour in the UK, and in France, the Socialist and Communist Parties plus sundry green, radical and extreme-left parties.

28. And these polarizations break on other lines too: female/male, non-white/white, metropolitan/provincial, and so on.

29. Hartman, Andrew. "The Culture Wars Are Dead." The Baffler, May 2018. Accessed May 22, 2020. https://thebaffler.

com/outbursts/culture-wars-are-dead-hartman.

30. Nagle, Angela. *Kill All Normies: Online Culture Wars from Tumblr and 4chan to the Alt-right and Trump*. Winchester: Zero Books, 2017.

31. This section draws on research by Morris P. Fiorina. *Unstable Majorities: Polarization, Party Sorting, and Political Stalemate*. Stanford, CA: Hoover Institution Press, Stanford University, 2017.

32. Solano, Esther, Pablo Ortellado and Márcio Moretto, "Guerras culturais e populismo antipetista nas manifestações por apoio à operação Lava Jato e contra a reforma de previdência," Belo Horizonte: UMFG, 2017. http://opiniaopublica.ufmg. br/site/files/artigo/7.pdf

Chapter 8

1. Seymour, Richard. "Bye Bye Labour." London Review of Books, November 7, 2019. https://www.lrb.co.uk/the-paper/ v37/n08/richard-seymour/bye-bye-labour.

2. Aufhebunga Bunga (/83/ Now It's Syrizous), *Aufhebunga Bunga* (podcast), September 12, 2019. https:// aufhebungabunga.podbean.com/e/83-now-it-s-syrizous-unlocked/.
   Rédaction. ""Le Corbynisme Est Mort" – Entretien Avec George Hoare." Le Vent Se Lève. October 3, 2019. https:// lvsl.fr/corbynisme-est-mort-entretien-avec-george-hoare/.

3. Cunliffe, Philip. "The Workers' Revolt Against Labour." The Full Brexit, December 18, 2019. https://www.thefullbrexit. com/workers-revolt-against-labour.

4. See: McCormack, Tara, and Lee Jones. "COVID-19 and the Failed Post-Political State." The Full Brexit, April 17, 2020. https://www.thefullbrexit.com/covid19-state-failure. Cunliffe, Philip, George Hoare, Lee Jones, and Peter Ramsey. "COVID-19: We're Not in Control." The Full Brexit, March 28, 2020. https://www.thefullbrexit.com/not-in-control.

5. Goodley, Simon, and Rupert Neate. "Leading US Bosses Drop Shareholder-first Principle." The Guardian, August 19, 2019. https://www.theguardian.com/business/2019/aug/19/leading-us-bosses-group-drops-principle-of-shareholder-first.

6. Editors. "25 Ideas That Will Shape the 2020s." Fortune, January 15, 2020. https://fortune.com/longform/ideas-shape-2020s-tech-economy-markets-ai-health-work-society/.

7. "The New Agenda." About the FT. Accessed January 20, 2020. https://aboutus.ft.com/en-gb/new-agenda/.

8. Cited in: Bagehot. "Boris Johnson Is Reinventing One-nation Conservatism." The Economist, January 2, 2020. https://www.economist.com/britain/2020/01/02/boris-johnson-is-reinventing-one-nation-conservatism.

9. For an example of an argument that proposes moving beyond the traditional class and regional links of the British Labour Party, see: Beckett, Andy. "Labour's Heartlands May Be Gone for Ever. It Needs to Find New Ones," The Guardian, January 11, 2020. https://www.theguardian.com/commentisfree/2020/jan/11/labour-heartlands-gone-away-northern-towns.

10. Krein, Julius. "The Real Class War." American Affairs Journal, November 21, 2019. https://americanaffairsjournal.org/2019/11/the-real-class-war/.

11. Really, a party of the provincial petty bourgeoisie with working-class support.

12. Slobodian, Quinn. "When the Green New Deal Goes Global." Foreign Policy, January 11, 2020. https://foreignpolicy.com/2020/01/11/green-new-deal-climate-planet-to-win-book-review/.

13. Hodgson, Camilla. "Citizens' Assembly Set to Offer UK Government Climate Advice." Financial Times, January 22, 2020. https://www.ft.com/content/788cccb6-3c4f-11ea-a01a-bae547046735.

The fact this was initiated by the Conservative government need not impede the Left to push for more. Indeed, this recapitulates the point about parasitism, made above.

14. Thompson, Matthew. "What's so New about New Municipalism?" *Progress in Human Geography*, March 9, 2020. doi:10.1177/0309132520909480.

15. Aaron Bastani (/72/ Frankly Awesome Lefty Conversation), *Aufhebunga Bunga* (podcast), May 30, 2019. https://aufhebungabunga.podbean.com/e/72-frankly-awesome-lefty-conversation-ft-aaron-bastani-unlocked/. Aufhebunga Bunga (/76/ CaliBunga: Tech, Drugs and Capitalist Soul, pt. 1), *Aufhebunga Bunga* (podcast). June 20, 2019. https://aufhebungabunga.podbean.com/e/76-calibunga-tech-drugs-capitalist-soul-pt-i/.

16. Morozov, Evgeny, *To Save Everything, Click Here: Technology, solutionism, and the urge to fix problems that don't exist*. London: Penguin, 2013.

17. Greenfield, Adam, *Radical Technologies: The Design of Everyday Life*. London: Verso, 2017.

18. Guilluy, Christophe, *Twilight of the Elites: Prosperity, the Periphery, and the Future of France*, London: Yale University Press, 2019, p. 96.

19. Hochuli, Alex. "Bolsonaro Rising." The Baffler, October 29, 2018. https://thebaffler.com/latest/bolsonaro-rising-hochuli.

About the Authors

The authors are co-producers and co-hosts of the global politics podcast Aufhebunga Bunga.

ALEX HOCHULI is a writer and research consultant based in São Paulo, Brazil, whose writing on Brazilian and global politics has appeared in publications including Jacobin, The Baffler, NBC, and Damage. Alex has degrees in international relations and in sociology from the LSE, King's College London and the University of Kent. He tweets @Alex__1789.

GEORGE HOARE is a researcher and writer based in London, UK. He holds a doctorate from the University of Oxford and has previously held research and teaching positions at Hertford College, Oxford, Leiden University College, and Fudan University in Shanghai. He is the co-author of *An Introduction to Antonio Gramsci* (Bloomsbury, 2016), and tweets @gtbho.

PHILIP CUNLIFFE is a Senior Lecturer in Politics and International Relations at the University of Kent. He joined the university in 2009 after completing his doctoral studies at King's College London. His research focuses on IR theory, international conflict management and liberal intervention. He appears frequently on radio and writes widely on politics, contributing to academic journals, reviews, business intelligence services, magazines and various political blogs. His other books include most recently *The New Twenty Years Crisis: A critique of international relations* (2020). He tweets @thephilippics.

Note to the Reader

You have reached the end of The End of the End of History.

The ideas put forward in the book will continue to be debated and developed on Aufhebunga Bunga. Our aim is to investigate politics around the globe – high and low, from international relations to subcultural trends – looking for the return of politics, as the neoliberal order crumbles. As well as long-form interviews and discussions, we also produce multi-episode docu-series exploring specific topics in depth.

Around half our episodes are for patrons only, which include a regular Reading Club and other original content. You can sign up at patreon.com/bungacast.

Episodes and written content can be found at bungacast.com

We can be reached on aufhebungabunga@gmail.com as well as via social media:

Facebook.com/bungacast

Twitter.com/bungacast

Instragram.com/bungacast

CULTURE, SOCIETY & POLITICS

The modern world is at an impasse. Disasters scroll across our smartphone screens and we're invited to like, follow or upvote, but critical thinking is harder and harder to find. Rather than connecting us in common struggle and debate, the internet has sped up and deepened a long-standing process of alienation and atomization. Zer0 Books wants to work against this trend. With critical theory as our jumping off point, we aim to publish books that make our readers uncomfortable. We want to move beyond received opinions.

Zer0 Books is on the left and wants to reinvent the left. We are sick of the injustice, the suffering and the stupidity that defines both our political and cultural world, and we aim to find a new foundation for a new struggle.

If this book has helped you to clarify an idea, solve a problem or extend your knowledge, you may want to check out our online content as well. Look for Zer0 Books: Advancing Conversations in the iTunes directory and for our Zer0 Books YouTube channel.

Popular videos include:

Žižek and the Double Blackmain

The Intellectual Dark Web is a Bad Sign

Can there be an Anti-SJW Left?

Answering Jordan Peterson on Marxism

Follow us on Facebook
at https://www.facebook.com/ZeroBooks and Twitter at https://
twitter.com/Zer0Books

Bestsellers from Zer0 Books include:

Give Them An Argument
Logic for the Left
Ben Burgis
Many serious leftists have learned to distrust talk of logic. This is
a serious mistake.
Paperback: 978-1-78904-210-8 ebook: 978-1-78904-211-5

Poor but Sexy
Culture Clashes in Europe East and West
Agata Pyzik
How the East stayed East and the West stayed West.
Paperback: 978-1-78099-394-2 ebook: 978-1-78099-395-9

An Anthropology of Nothing in Particular
Martin Demant Frederiksen
A journey into the social lives of meaninglessness.
Paperback: 978-1-78535-699-5 ebook: 978-1-78535-700-8

In the Dust of This Planet
Horror of Philosophy vol. 1
Eugene Thacker
In the first of a series of three books on the Horror of Philosophy,
In the Dust of This Planet offers the genre of horror as a way of
thinking about the unthinkable.
Paperback: 978-1-84694-676-9 ebook: 978-1-78099-010-1

The End of Oulipo?
An Attempt to Exhaust a Movement
Lauren Elkin, Veronica Esposito
Paperback: 978-1-78099-655-4 ebook: 978-1-78099-656-1

Capitalist Realism
Is There No Alternative?
Mark Fisher
An analysis of the ways in which capitalism has presented itself
as the only realistic political-economic system.
Paperback: 978-1-84694-317-1 ebook: 978-1-78099-734-6

Rebel Rebel
Chris O'Leary
David Bowie: every single song. Everything you want to know,
everything you didn't know.
Paperback: 978-1-78099-244-0 ebook: 978-1-78099-713-1

Kill All Normies
Angela Nagle
Online culture wars from 4chan and Tumblr to Trump.
Paperback: 978-1- 78535-543-1 ebook: 978-1-78535-544-8

Romeo and Juliet in Palestine
Teaching Under Occupation
Tom Sperlinger
Life in the West Bank, the nature of pedagogy and the role of a
university under occupation.
Paperback: 978-1-78279-637-4 ebook: 978-1-78279-636-7

Ghosts of My Life
Writings on Depression, Hauntology and Lost Futures
Mark Fisher
Paperback: 978-1-78099-226-6 ebook: 978-1-78279-624-4

Sweetening the Pill
or How We Got Hooked on Hormonal Birth Control
Holly Grigg-Spall
Has contraception liberated or oppressed women?
Sweetening the Pill breaks the silence on the dark side of hormonal
contraception.
Paperback: 978-1-78099-607-3 ebook: 978-1-78099-608-0

Why Are We The Good Guys?
Reclaiming Your Mind from the Delusions of Propaganda
David Cromwell
A provocative challenge to the standard ideology that Western
power is a benevolent force in the world.
Paperback: 978-1-78099-365-2 ebook: 978-1-78099-366-9

The Writing on the Wall
On the Decomposition of Capitalism and its Critics
Anselm Jappe, Alastair Hemmens
A new approach to the meaning of social emancipation.
Paperback: 978-1-78535-581-3 ebook: 978-1-78535-582-0

Enjoying It
Candy Crush and Capitalism
Alfie Bown
A study of enjoyment and of the enjoyment of studying. Bown
asks what enjoyment says about us and what we say about
enjoyment, and why.
Paperback: 978-1-78535-155-6 ebook: 978-1-78535-156-3

Color, Facture, Art and Design
Iona Singh
This materialist definition of fine-art develops guidelines for
architecture, design, cultural-studies and ultimately social
change.
Paperback: 978-1-78099-629-5 ebook: 978-1-78099-630-1

Neglected or Misunderstood
The Radical Feminism of Shulamith Firestone
Victoria Margree
An interrogation of issues surrounding gender, biology,
sexuality, work and technology, and the ways in which our
imaginations continue to be in thrall to ideologies of maternity
and the nuclear family.
Paperback: 978-1-78535-539-4 ebook: 978-1-78535-540-0

How to Dismantle the NHS in 10 Easy Steps (Second Edition)
Youssef El-Gingihy
The story of how your NHS was sold off and why you will have
to buy private health insurance soon. A new expanded second
edition with chapters on junior doctors' strikes and government
blueprints for US-style healthcare.
Paperback: 978-1-78904-178-1 ebook: 978-1-78904-179-8

Digesting Recipes
The Art of Culinary Notation
Susannah Worth
A recipe is an instruction, the imperative tone of the expert, but
this constraint can offer its own kind of potential. A recipe need
not be a domestic trap but might instead offer escape – something
to fantasise about or aspire to.

Paperback: 978-1-78279-860-6 ebook: 978-1-78279-859-0